Development Financing

Two volumes from the Centre for Research on the
New International Economic Order, Oxford:

Volume 1
International Financial Cooperation — A Framework
Frances Stewart and Arjun Sengupta
Edited by Salah Al-Shaikhly

Volume 2
**Development Financing — A Framework for
International Financial Cooperation**
Edited by Salah Al-Shaikhly

Development Financing

A Framework for International
Financial Co-operation

Editor
Salah Al-Shaikhly

Frances Pinter (Publishers), London
Westview Press, Boulder, Colorado

© The Centre for Research on the New International
Economic Order, Oxford, 1982

First published in Great Britain in 1982 by
Frances Pinter (Publishers) Limited
5 Dryden Street, London WC2E 9NW

ISBN 0 86187 237 1

Published in 1982 in the United States of America by
Westview Press, 5500 Central Ave.
Boulder, Colorado, 80301
Frederick A. Praeger, Publisher

ISBN 0-86531-417-9

Library of Congress No. 82-80427

British Library Cataloguing in Publication Data

Development financing.
    1.   Economic assistance   2.   Underdeveloped
    Areas — Finance
    I.   Al-Shaikhly, Salah
    3384.91'172'4   HC 60

    ISBN 0-86187-237-1

Typeset by Anne Joshua Associates, Oxford
Printed by SRP, Exeter, Great Britain

TABLE OF CONTENTS

ACKNOWLEDGEMENTS

The Centre for Research on the New International Economic Order gratefully acknowledges the contributions of Dr Dragoslav Avramovic, whose paper appears as Chapter 1 of this book, for developing the idea behind this project and giving it firm and clear dimensions. The papers in this volume were part of the project sponsored by the United Nations Development Programme (The Bureau for Arab States). These papers were selected to represent various points of view and the Centre is grateful to the authors for their contributions, especially those, who in spite of their other engagements, had to meet our deadlines.

We would also like to acknowledge the assistance of Alan Robinson and Platon Tinios in the research work, editing and compilation of the final report in this project.

Finally we must mention Frances Pinter and Anne Joshua for their remarkable job of arranging the proof reading, printing and production of the book within a short period of receiving the manuscripts. This has facilitated our aim of keeping the research community informed of the Centre's work in a regular and timely fashion.

FOREWORD

This book constitutes what can be seen as the second volume to a previous publication, *International Financial Cooperation — A Framework* by Frances Stewart and Arjun Sengupta. During the process of this research work the Centre invited and received some fifteen excellent research papers from professors, politicians and practitioners in the field of International Finance. During the process of preparing the original document we managed to extract ideas and proposals that were basically contained in these papers and bring them out in Volume One. We found it necessary, however, to give some examples of the quality of work and contributions that were made during the process of preparing the original document.

The papers in this edition were chosen to represent three distinct points of view on the subject of International Financial Cooperation. The first view is that which favours the traditional OPEC point of view which has emerged in various international forums since 1974. The second point of view is that which has been advanced by the Non-Oil Developing Countries. This view was advanced by researchers and politicians from Asia and Africa. The third point of view is that of the North (Europe/U.S.A.). It is in accordance with the principles and Charter of the Centre, to present the current prevailing points of view, that we have undertaken this task. The Centre believes that debate can only be useful if there are a variety of views and proposals. We will endeavour to maintain these standards and even promote them through our research and seminar programmes.

Dr. Salah Al-Shaikhly
Director
Centre for Research on the New International Economic Order
Oxford

INTRODUCTION
International Financial Cooperation
The Hurdle in Global Negotiations

The introduction to Volume One of this edition ended with a note on Cancun. By necessity that note was a quick response to the communiqué coming out of the conference. Since then sufficient details have been available to assemble a more accurate assessment of what to expect beyond Cancun. Nevertheless certain initial impressions still hold valid. The meeting was projected as being neither a complete success nor a complete failure. There was, however, sufficient evidence to suggest that, in principle, an understanding had been reached to initiate the next round of the global negotiations.

In the past few years the problem was not whether or not to negotiate, but rather where and what to negotiate. The North (read USA, Germany and the UK) was uneasy about the procedural and agenda aspects of the proposed global negotiations. The South wanted the negotiations to take place at the United Nations General Assembly with all the countries participating in the dialogue. The South also felt that the crucial issues of food and agriculture, trade and industry, energy and finance should be included in the agenda. The North felt that the UN General Assembly was not the proper forum to tackle these issues. The North argued further that as far as the question of trade, industry and finance is concerned, the World Bank, the IMF and GATT are the only qualified institutions with the competence to discuss these issues. At the heart of the disagreement is the voting structure in the UN General Assembly and the other three institutions. The UN General Assembly is constituted on the basis of one country, one vote, and the developing countries form an overwhelming majority. On the other hand the voting structure in the other three institutions is weighted in favour of the North.

It is obvious that neither side is going to change its position as long as the other side has such a distinct advantage. The solution obviously must lie somewhere in the middle of these two proposals. It has been suggested that perhaps the Economic and Social Council of the UN can provide a suitable forum with some appropriate adjustments to the numbers of participating countries for each group.

We must remember that, in the final analysis, the UN members are sovereign countries and any resolution that is thought to be contrary to the country's immediate interest will never be implemented. The fate of many UN resolutions since 1945 would support this point.

Of the four basic issues that were thrown open for general debate at Cancun, food and agriculture proved to be the least controversial. On the other hand, the question of finance, which includes development financing and debt servicing, is one of the most crucial issues not only in Cancun but also in all North–South relations. It was not expected that any tangible conclusions would be reached at Cancun on the question of finance and consequently very little was done apart from identifying the underlying causes of the problem. Even here there were, and still are, a number of misconceptions about the predicament of the South. For example, a temporary balance-of-payments deficit can be met with the help of the international financial institutions or even through bilateral and private means. The problem, however, is not a temporary one and will not go away with the one-off kind of operation.

The debt problem of developing countries is a structural one and is not a temporary phenomena related to a given period of time or certain events or crises. Many studies have shown that the present global crisis is the result of over three decades of abuse of the global economic system. The emphasis here is therefore that the whole framework of international exchange and finance must be renegotiated with the aim of being readjusted in such a way as to induce greater participation by the developing countries in the management and decision-making process. In Volume 1, a number of proposals were put forward for short- and long- term remedies of the financial problems of LDCs. In Cancun, yet another proposal was made by the Austrian delegation, which was reminiscent of the old Marshall Plan. The proposal entailed the transfer of about $14 billion per year over the next fifteen years to developing countries.

Problems of Negotiations on Finance

By definition, negotiating on any issue means that the negotiating sides have a certain amount of leverage one way or another. This definition is just as valid in the context of global negotiations. In the past, the North and South did hold negotiations on such issues as price stabilization and commodities, and in each of these each side started from a different vantage point. In the area of finance the basis is quite different from those of commodities, for example. In the area of negotiating on finance, the South seems to be at a disadvantage from the very beginning. On the other hand, the presence of OPEC amongst the developing countries could be regarded as a source of negotiating strength to developing countries. For the past eight years the OPEC countries have been at the forefront of events when furthering the cause of the South. Nevertheless, OPEC strength aside, most developing countries feel that their negotiating leverage must be derived from the significant role they play in the working of the global economy. Internal economic measures taken in the industrialized countries — — like the increase of interest rates, the cut in public expenditure, wage restriction, etc. — have not only affected these countries themselves, but have also had adverse effects on many of the developing countries. Unfortunately the realities of such interdependence are not always reflected in the perception of the North, and many of the financial problems of the LDCs are seen in the industrialized countries as normal trade deficit that can be remedied thrrough the existing financial institutions. In many cases the Western media portrays any such interdependence as situations worthy of acts of charity rather than serious matters that are threatening the present global economic system. At no time during the past few years of rising unemployment, inflation and rates of interest, have the industrial countries appreciated the structural linkage between their own economies and those of the developing countries. For this reason any attempt to increase assistance or transfer of more resources or adjust the present structure of the international financial institutions has met with some apprehension from the taxpayer in the industrial countries. The question of development finance and debt servicing is not purely a technical one which be easily overcome by advancing a few plausible solutions.

The Argument for Change

Unfortunately, whenever the word debt in developing countries is mentioned the first thing that comes to mind is its association with the rising oil bill in these countries. However, the Lester Pearson Commission, whose report came out long before the oil crisis, estimated that in 1977 the servicing of debt would alone exceed the total amount of new loans to developing countries by 20 per cent in Africa, and 30 per cent in Latin America. In other words, a developing country can hardly borrow any funds for development if such funds go towards paying the interest on previous loans. Looking as far back as 1960, the external national debt of developing countries came to several billion dollars. During the 1960s the total indebtedness of some eighty developing countries was rising at an annual rate of 14 per cent to about 59 billion dollars at the beginning of 1970. During the same period the total sums dispersed by these countries simply to cover the servicing of the national debt and the repatriation of profits were estimated at 11 billion dollars. In fact a number of developing countries have been paying what amounts to 20 per cent of their total export revenue to debt servicing. Of course the economic crises from 1973 onwards have added to the problems of developing countries who are highly dependent for their imports and have increased their external debt accordingly. It is interesting to note that the average rate of inflation for 1962–72 was 4 per cent in most industrialized countries. This rose to 7 per cent in 1973, 12 per cent in 1974, and remained at that level until 1978–9. The rate of inflation in countries like the United Kingdom and Japan was over 20 per cent in 1975. The picture in non-oil exporting countries is also very alarming. Their deficit rose from 9.1 billion dollars in 1973 to 27.5 billion in 1974 and 35 billion in 1976. These deficits obviously caused a massive rise in the outstanding external indebtedness of the developing countries and the servicing on the debt for 1974/5. Unfortunately proposals and solutions put forward by the developing countries to correct these imbalances did not get the approval of the industrialized creditor countries. The debtor countries made it perfectly clear that, for most of them, the burden of indebtedness was such that if the position were not reviewed any hope of development in these countries might well be terminated. Needless to say, the argument still goes on, and the Cancun summit seems to have done very little to bring about any North–South consensus on these issues.

1 OPEN ISSUES IN INTERNATIONAL FINANCE

Dragoslav Avramovic

The problems in early 1980

Six problem areas now exist in international finance.

First, there are major gaps in the present institutional structure of organized international development finance. These gaps severely hamper the growth process of developing countries, and some of them threaten the stability and growth of developed countries as well. The elements which are substantially missing are: finance for development programmes as a whole (programme finance); commodity stabilization and related finance; export finance, particularly for capital goods; finance for energy and mineral development; finance for supporting economic cooperation amongst developing countries; and finance for debt reorganization. In addition, finance for industrial investment in developing countries is inadequate.

Secondly, the fundamental imbalance in international payments persists, as reflected in a simultaneous existence of large surpluses of a few countries and large deficits of many others. The aggregate deficit of the non-oil developing countries is growing sharply. Unless measures are taken to assure the use of surpluses for long-term international investment, the ongoing deflationary and trade-restricting policies may be further tightened and affect incomes and employment everywhere. A break in the post-war expansionary trend in the developed countries has occurred, and unused plant capacity is substantial in a number of sectors. In the developing countries there is a danger of deceleration of growth, mainly due to the foreign-exchange constraint.

Thirdly, it is unlikely that the international private banking system which had played a crucial role in channelling the surpluses to the deficit countries in the last six years, would be able to perform this role on the same scale in the future. The foreign exposure of major US banks which had spearheaded the international credit drive in the 1970s, has increased enormously and further expansion will be much slower: by 1976 more than one-half of total profits of ten leading US banks were derived from foreign operations compared to less than one-quarter five years earlier; and in 1977 as much as two-thirds and four-fifths of total profits of the two leading New York banks consisted of foreign earnings. In France, between 40 and 50 per cent of the profits of the two leading private banks were earned abroad in recent years. In the Federal Republic of Germany, one-third of the assets of the three leading private banks consisted of loans to developing countries and Eastern Europe in 1978. Only in the Japanese banks is foreign business as a proportion of the total still relatively small and they are now expanding rapidly, but it is unlikely that the rate of expansion will match that of the US banks recorded in recent years. While there are no automatic or rigid limits to foreign exposure, the perception of risk has risen as the external deficits of the non-oil developing countries, after a decline in 1977 and 1978, have again turned sharply upwards and are expected to increase further. The burden of their financing is now superimposed on an already heavy debt structure of which the banks hold a substantial share — a situation different from that in the early and mid-1970s.

Fourthly, the international monetary system is in disarray, with major adverse repercussions on international trade and investment. The decline of the US dollar as the key reserve currency has affected the real value not only of current income of the exporting countries, but also of financial assets held in this currency. This is of particular importance for countries exporting exhaustible resources and accumulating financial assets: in periods of inflation and exchange-rate depreciation of reserve currencies, these countries will experience a net loss of national wealth unless offsetting measures of an international nature are taken. Furthermore, no government is now committed to support, in case of emergency, the substantial part of the international banking structure which has been permitted to expand enormously in recent years without any restraints and safeguards customary in national banking regulations. There are great uncertainties concerning the future value of the main reserve currency and the future supply of other potential reserve currencies. The volume of liquidity in the world economy is now decided in the lottery of gold prices. The need for a planned and controlled expansion of international reserve assets has probably never been greater.

Fifthly, the developing countries do not have an adequate share of responsibility for decision-making, control and management of most of the existing international financial and monetary institutions. While these institutions have made a significant contribution through their loans and technical assistance, they have not provided adequate support to some of the activities which the developing countries have considered of crucial importance — hence the gaps in the financing structure listed above. Also, there are deep misgivings concerning the involvement of some of these institutions in the determination of policies and priorities of developing countries, which has frequently gone beyond what could be justified on grounds of safety of loans and their adequate use.

Finally, the international financial and monetary institutions are not universal. The USSR and most of the socialist countries are not members, and China has so far abstained from taking its place in these institutions. The lack of universality, in addition to its political cost, deprives countries of the benefits of mutual development experience and curtails the scope of international assistance.

It is against this background of the growing world economic and financial crisis and institutional deficiencies that the issues of reform and restructuring of the international financial system and institutions have to be approached. The persistent imbalance of international payments, the need for world-wide investment to stimulate the world economy, and the growing recognition of the need for major measures in international finance provide a unique opportunity for an international effort which would simultaneously close the gaps in the financing structure, raise employment and income, meet the legitimate demands of the surplus countries for the maintenance of the real value of their assets, and constitute a major step towards a new international economic order.

The remainder of this note deals with the first problem area — the gaps.

The gaps in the financing structure

Programme finance is needed to provide support for the entire set of projects and activities of a country, and help ensure their execution in the face of fluctuating fiscal revenue and balance of payments. It is not tied to specific projects, but assists the development programme as a whole. It is needed on terms compatible with the long-run nature of most investments and the time required to correct structural imbalances in the external accounts of developing countries. Such finance is not available now on satisfactory terms. The IMF assistance which supports stabilization programmes or offsets shortfalls in export earnings is of short and medium maturity and is not a substitute for long-term programme lending. Under these conditions, the developing countries have turned to massive borrowing from private banks which have provided the needed funds to countries considered acceptable risks, but mostly on short and medium term. The result has been the shortening of the debt structure and a massive roll-over problem for a number of borrowers. On the other hand, the weaker and the poorer developing countries have not been able to obtain private bank finance, but have had to rely almost exclusively on external project finance supplied by official assistance agencies. The disbursement of external project loans has been very slow, reducing their effectiveness. The constraints on the expansion of international bank credit, the risks involved in the present unbalanced debt structure and insufficient access to credit not tied to projects for a large number of poorer countries call for long-term programme lending on a substantial scale, equivalent in importance to project lending. The major problem in official programme loans has been the economic policy conditions, which have been normally related to the size and composition of investment and the adequacy of domestic resource mobilization. These issues are more critical for the success of the development effort of a country than is the successful execution of a single project under a project loan. But these are issues which affect very deeply the income and employment levels, the priorities, and income distribution in developing countries — all highly political subjects. They can be resolved without causing major frictions between lenders and borrowers only if the latter are assured full and equal participation in setting the lending conditions and in implementing them.

Commodity stabilization and related finance is needed to assure a price floor for export primary products of developing countries. Such a floor is a condition for improvements in their terms of trade and debt-servicing capacity. The price floor would also help sustain world effective demand for manufactured goods. The need for commodity stabilization finance has been recognized for a long time, but no decisive action has been taken and the pervasive instability of commodity prices continues to be a source of dislocation in the world economy. Especially vulnerable are the weak economies heavily dependent on a few primary exports. The UNCTAD Integrated Programme for Commodities, with the Common Fund as its central element, was formulated in response to this need. The negotiations on the Programme and the Fund are still under way. Only one commodity agreement has been concluded under the Programme so far, and a preliminary agreement on the principal elements of the Common Fund was reached in early 1979. The latter agreement envisages a different capitalization and financing structure than was originally proposed, and for the Fund to exercise a catalytic effect on concluding new commodity agreements it will need a larger capital support when negotiated or increased programme lending to meet the needs or financing of international stocks, national stocks and diversification and productivity improvements.

The developing countries need support in providing *export credit finance*, particularly for capital goods. A number of these countries are now exporting such goods in rising quantities, with others establishing the potential to do so.

These sales often require extension of medium-term credit which the developing countries' exporters must provide and for which, being mostly deficit countries, they need re-financing. Many initiatives to establish such refinancing schemes have not been followed by lending agencies. Only the Inter-American Development Bank has a refinancing facility limited to capital goods sales mainly within the region, and a recently established Latin American Export Credit Bank, with an equity participation by the International Finance Corporation, plans to refinance short- and medium-term credit for non-traditional goods. One of the effects of instituting a programme of broad support for export credit finance for developing countries, which is now lacking, would be to stimulate trade amongst them. Another effect would be the diversification of the export structure of developing countries.

There is no need for *finance to support economic coopera-tion* amongst developing countries, especially in the form of assistance for their payments arrangements aimed at increasing their general intra-trade. Better export finance for capital goods would contribute to it, but the needs are broader. Expansion of general trade through market integration arrangements has long been an important method of coopera-tion among the developing countries. That a number of integrated schemes have achieved only slow progress, or have encountered retrogression, has been due in part to balance of payments difficulties experienced by one or more of the participants. Mutual credit extension through payments arrangements would be the principal means of overcoming the difficulty and thus accelerating integration. However, there will be need for external assistance. It arises when those group members with intra-group surpluses experience difficult overall payments positions, and have highly restricted access to external sources of finance and are hence reluctant to accentuate their own difficulties by extending credits to the deficit members. More generally, there will be need for the periodic settlement of balances from intra-trade, which will need support of outside finance. Furthermore, outside finance will be needed for large joint investment projects. Intensified trade amongst developing countries, as a part of

their general economic cooperation, is of particular importance under present international economic circumstances in
view of the slow growth in industrialized countries and
increased protectionism. It would contribute both to accelerated growth in developing countries and to the widening of
the world market, thus helping the world economic recovery
including the recovery in the industrialized countries.

An expansion is needed in *energy and mineral finance*. The
traditional pattern of oil and mineral (non-fuel) finance and
exploitation, which was dominated by the international oil
and mining companies providing capital, bearing exploration
risks, operating 'enclave' projects and taking most of the
profits and rents, has now broken down, and the need
for a new regime of exploiting natural resources is widely
recognized. The almost complete absorption of profits and
rents has been a cause of great and continuing resentment in
the countries where oil and mineral deposits were found;
while the companies argued that extra profits were justified
in part because of exploration risks. It was the initial unequal
bargaining strength of developing countries which frequently
led to subsequent investment disputes. What is of crucial
importance is the strengthening of their bargaining capacity,
which comes with the diversification of the sources of
finance, and of technical and marketing knowledge, especially
at the time of investment, if minerals are to be exploited
with satisfactory benefits for these countries and at a rate
needed by the world economy. As part of the new regime,
international sharing of exploration risks is needed. International development banks had traditionally abstained
from lending for oil and minerals, essentially leaving these
fields to private investment. The situation is now changing
and these banks are lending or planning to lend for projects
in these areas; but the lending plans are small in relation to
the needs. Without adequate support from organized public
finance, resources are unlikely to be developed; in many
cases mineral projects in developing countries have a higher
rate of return (mineral deposits in developing countries are
richer) than in developed areas, but investment has been
lagging. The developing countries need to have an adequate
participation in the control and management of the organized

finance if they are to be on equal negotiating footing with transnational companies.

Accelerated industrialization of developing countries, as called for in the Lima target (25 per cent of world industrial production to be located in these countries by the year 2000, compared to 7 per cent in 1975 when the target was formulated), will have to be supported by large-scale borrowing of *industrial finance* from official long-term sources. In the past only some ten to fifteen developing countries have received significant direct investment in industry by transnational corporations. Previously most developing countries have financed industrial investment through export credits from the industrialized countries and by borrowing from banks; but the repayment terms have been short, bank credit has frequently been very expensive and export credits have been available for financing only the foreign-exchange cost of projects. The poorer countries, as noted, have had only limited access to private funds. Most official aid has gone to such purposes as agriculture and infrastructure, and industry has not received adequate support. For a long time international development banks refused to finance government-owned industry altogether; they have recently made more finance available for industry, but this is only a fraction of rapidly rising needs.

Debt reorganization finance is needed to help countries in serious and sustained debt servicing difficulties. The debt servicing record of developing countries has been excellent on the whole, particularly *vis-à-vis* private banks, but there have been debt servicing difficulties and occasionally payments crises, resulting from reckless borrowing as well as from causes beyond debtor's control. With rising debts and a growing number of debtors these difficulties are likely to increase. The past case-by-case approach to handling debt problems has been unsatisfactory. In most instances, the concerned creditors have worked out a debt rescheduling within the framework of so-called clubs, with only the near-term debt being refinanced on terms which have often resulted in severe constraints on debtor's development ('short-leash' approach), making it difficult for him to engage in long-term investment and production plans and policies which would restore the debt servicing capacity on a sustained basis. Creditors' claims have in most cases been protected in full, even when they have shared the responsibility for the crisis, having imposed unfair terms in original contracts on government operating in financial distress or ignorance. Neither principles nor machinery for debt refinancing now exist. While in a number of cases the debt profile can be improved through new borrowing on terms better than the existing debt, this remedy is unlikely to be sufficient in difficult debt cases where an overhaul of the debt is needed through a rearrangement of the entire maturity structure and a renegotiation of interest. Such cases call for a debt refinancing facility which would either assume the debt on renegotiated terms and substitute for the earlier creditors or guarantee repayment of the renegotiated amounts. As a part of the refinancing operation, agreement would have to be reached with the debtor on a short- and long-term plan aimed at restoring economic growth and balance of payments viability, and avoiding debt difficulties in the future. The facility should be such as to inspire the confidence both of the creditors and the debtor, and of the international community at large.

General

The financing gaps discussed above are not a new discovery. The world economy has experienced their effects for decades, and the developing countries have made major efforts to convince the lenders of the need for closing the gaps. This refers in particular to programme lending and commodity stabilization finance, but also to others. These efforts have been successful only to a very limited extent. The development literature has recognized the existence of these gaps and largely agreed on the need for new initiatives to close them, but practical action has lagged badly. What has perhaps not been sufficiently realized is that these different gaps have one common feature: they go to the heart of the economic and political relationships between the developed and developing countries. Whether it is programme lending, commodity stabilization, promotion of developing countries' exports, finance to enable them to cooperate with each other more effectively, the development of their energy and mineral resources to their best advantage, their accelerated industrialization, or the reorganization of unviable debt structures, all these in their several ways, singly and together, are forms and types of finance which would enable poor countries to become self-reliant and independent participants in a more equitable exchange with the rich countries. Thus they all call for a new approach to decision-making. It is this approach which has so far been lacking in North–South relations and which has so far defeated various efforts towards reform of the existing international financial system on covering these gaps.

What is necessary is to examine in detail the nature of the gaps; examine the various proposals for resource transfers and their organization which have recently been made; and then suggest the institutional solutions to meet the needs and fill the gaps.

Addendum

This article was written in February 1980. The events since have largely confirmed the analysis, with some modifications.

(a) Most of the gaps in the structure of organized finance have remained essentially unfilled, although important steps have been taken to meet some of them (see further below).

(b) The fundamental imbalance in international payments has not been removed. The current account deficit of oil-importing developing countries, estimated at $70 billion for 1980, turned out to be $80 billion (IMF estimate); in 1981 it is likely to run at $90 billion (IMF) to $97 billion (Group of Twenty-four estimate); and in 1982 it should move to the $100–110 billion level. As debt amortization requirements are now running at $40–50 billion p.a., the aggregate needs for finance of these countries are some $150 billion p.a. this year and the next.

(c) The international banking system, which has done a

remarkable job in recycling, above the expectations of many including this author, will have to operate under increasing strain in view of the large, and growing, exposure of the key banks in some major debtor countries. An unfinanced gap is likely to remain, despite the reduction of investment and income growth targets in many cases. It is the low-income and the over-stretched mid-income countries which would be particularly affected if the gap is not filled. The effects, economic, social and political, may, under certain circumstances, be far-reaching over vast areas of the globe, in both the free-enterprise and the socialist developing countries; and the banks, and the government budgets, in developed countries may not be saved from them.

(d) The disarray in international monetary affairs has experienced a new twist: competition in interest rates, with immediate effects on exchange rates, commodity markets, and the position of weaker enterprises and countries. The fight against inflation − an important element neglected in the February 1980 analysis − has become nearly universal; and raising the rate of interest has become a key policy tool in most market economies. As a large proportion of the debt of developing countries was contracted at floating interest rates in recent years (probably some $200 billion), their upward shift raises sharply the debt service payments. A one percentage point increase in the rate raises this service, and the current account deficit, by $2 billion per year. Similarly, an increase in the price of imported oil of $1 per barrel, raises the import bill by $1.5 billion p.a. Added to this is the fact that the export commodity prices of non-oil developing countries are probably at their lowest level, in real terms, since 1950. The saving grace is that the prices of grains, now a major import of developing countries, have not been raised to any significant degree in recent years: otherwise we would have had a catastrophy in many places.

(e) No significant change has occurred in the decision-making structure of most international financial and monetary institutions. This issue is gradually moving to the centre of global negotiations. They are now suspended pending the Mexico North–South summit organized at the initiative of the Brandt Commission and scheduled for October 1981 to deal with the most urgent and important issues.

(f) A major step forward in the direction of the universality of the Bretton Woods institutions has occurred: China has joined. Rumours are that Poland may also come in, but such rumours, with respect to one or another Eastern European country, have cropped up frequently in the past, without a follow-up. The crux of the matter is whether an agreement is possible between the Western countries and the USSR, which would result in a universal system of financial, monetary and trade institutions. This issue is part of a much broader complex of East–West relations. From the present vantage point, such an agreement is improbable. However, the world economic situation is potentially so bad and the burden of armaments so crushing, that the possible social and political effects of both may convince most countries and regimes that an agreement is vital for the self-preservation of everybody.

A final word on the gaps in the financing structure — (a) above. In programme (non-project) lending, the IMF provided to developing countries recently amounts unheard of before (Yugoslavia $1.9 billion, Turkey 1.8, Pakistan 1.1, Korea 0.8, Bangladesh 0.6; amounts rumoured for India and Brazil range from $5 to $5 billion each), and apparently on reasonable economic policy conditions. The World Bank introduced a new type of long-term loans, for structural adjustment, which are quickly disbursing and thus can be a crucial supplement to its traditional project lending and can also boost the import capacity, if provided in substantial amounts. The programme so far is modest. The World Bank has also put forward a proposal for the establishment of an affiliate to provide investment finance for energy. The response to the proposal by some key countries has been cool or negative, but it is unlikely that this initiative will be permitted to collapse.

Work is being initiated in devising ways for meeting the gaps in export finance and in economic cooperation finance. The crucial issue here is the extent to which the surplus developing countries will find it possible to assist the rest, and this will depend on whether they feel that their long-term economic interests are satisfied.

No progress has been achieved in commodity stabilization. Individual commodity discussions have failed (except in rubber), and the Common Fund, as negotiated, now in the process of being signed and ratified, will not be able to provide effective assistance in the absence of such commodity agreements. In industrial finance, the UNIDO initiatives for major new facilities have not resulted in action so far. In agricultural finance — another field neglected in the February analysis — the IMF has established a food financing facility to compensate developing countries for balance of payments difficulties caused by an excess in their cost of cereals imports. Little has been done to increase the level of agricultural investment. Finally, no progress has been made in setting up finance for debt reorganization. *Ad hoc* deals are being arranged as crises strike, and they do with increasing frequency. No advance contingency planning and financial provisions are under way.

The initiatives of the World Bank and the IMF in programme, energy and agricultural lending are encouraging. Meanwhile, the deficit of the developing countries has grown, and new initiatives must be urgently considered. They are needed to relieve the rapidly growing financial, economic, social and political pressures; and they also provide the opportunity for a new deal in the North–South, and perhaps East–West, relations.

2 THE ROLE OF THE NEW OPEC DEVELOPMENT AGENCY

Abdelkader Sid Ahmed*

During the ordinary conference of OPEC ministers held at Caracas in 1979, Algeria and Venezuela submitted a proposal for the creation of a Third World Development Agency. Based on the practical lessons learnt from the functioning of the OPEC Provisional Special Fund since its creation in 1976, the proposal called for the transformation of this Fund into a permanent institution with full international legal status.

At the end of the conference an agreement was reached as to the necessity of transforming the OPEC Special Fund into a permanent body, endowed with appropriate powers. The Algerian–Venezuelan proposal was then submitted to the OPEC Technical Committee for Long-term Strategy, under the chairmanship of Zaki Yemani, the Saudi minister for petroleum. Already in 1978, OPEC petroleum ministers at Taif had asked Yemani to devise, with the help of experts from the member countries, a long-term strategy for the future course of petroleum prices, OPEC relations to other developing countries and OPEC's dialogue with the industrial countries. In June 1979, at the ministerial OPEC meeting held in Geneva, the Iraqi delegation submitted to the Technical Committee a proposal for the creation of a joint development fund involving the industrial countries, OPEC and other Third World countries.

Thus, at the February 1980 meeting in London, the Technical Committee for Long-term Strategy had before it two proposals concerning the question of OPEC's aid to other

* Ministry of Energy and Petrochemical Industries, Algiers.

developing countries. The earlier, Iraqi proposal, recommended a Joint Fund drawn from contributions worked out on the basis of the respective inflation rates in the developed countries as well as the rate of increase in the price of crude oil. The model for this Joint Fund was, for the Iraqis, the International Fund for Agricultural Development. As to the subsequent proposal by Algeria and Venezuela, it was essentially motivated by the need to reinforce collective self-reliance amongst developing countries and to directly recycle OPEC surpluses in the Third World.

Although these two proposals are at complementary levels, they nevertheless embody different philosophies. The Iraqi proposal presupposes implicitly that the urgent problems of the developing countries could be solved by finding new forms of aid from the developed countries. The Algerian–Venezuelan proposal, on the other hand, rests on the premise that, under the current international system of financial cooperation, the only course left for the Third World (of which OPEC is an integral part) is to strengthen its unity by promoting new financial mechanisms – like the recycling of existing surpluses directly into the Third World.

Be that as it may, in May 1980, at the special Taif meeting of OPEC ministers gathered to approve the report of the Technical Committee, both proposals were adopted without any qualification – emphasis being placed on the Algerian–Venezuelan proposal. In fact, as early as February 1980, OPEC finance ministers meeting in Vienna had directed a working party of the Technical Committee to plan the transformation of the OPEC Special Fund entirely 'along the broad guidelines of the Algerian–Venezuelan Proposal'.

However, on 27 May 1980 in Vienna, OPEC ministers decided to go ahead with the transformation of the OPEC Special Fund into a permanent fund with legal international status, without any regard for the recommendations of the Technical Committee. In so refusing to consider the Algerian–Venezuelan proposals for a reform of the Special Fund statutes, the intention of the majority of OPEC finance ministers was to limit the scope of the Fund's activities and keep its function as primarily one of providing traditional aid. On the basis of this decision by the finance ministers, the majority of the Technical Committee — which had been asked by the June 1980 Algiers meeting of petroleum ministers to formulate a programme for action based on the strategy report — blocked the Algerian–Venezuelan proposal. Hence, in the document outlining the programme of action to the tri-ministerial conference in Vienna (14–15 September), the Algerian–Venezuelan proposal was merely treated as a memorandum, whereas the Iraqi plans were considered at length — the argument being that since the transformation of the Fund had already been carried out, there was no need to discuss the Algerian–Venezuelan proposal for the new Agency.

Today, then, the situation appears to be deadlocked, though the proposal still stands intact. With the adoption of the Technical Committee report, the principal behind the Algerian–Venezuelan proposal has been retained (though not the exact amount of capital suggested). Nor does the insufficient modification of the Special Fund's structures cancel out the agreement reached in this respect — an agreement which defines the action of OPEC for the next 20 years. Besides, since the Iraqi and Algerian–Venezuelan proposals operate at different levels and concern different agents, they should not be counterposed to each other. The report of the Technical Committee itself recognizes their complementary character. Clearly, a financial policy based on financial mechanisms specifically related to the Third World does not exclude the existence of other financial mechanisms aiming at stronger international financial co-operation — quite the contrary.

For the moment, then, it could only be hoped that the second summit of OPEC heads of state and sovereigns will throw some light on this apparently confused situation. Nevertheless, in the meantime, in the face of the catastrophic economic situation of some Third World countries, it is clearly not enough for OPEC to simply renovate its past methods of action, however important a role OPEC activities may have played in the past. Unless policies could be devised for a more effective, systematic and general cooperation with, and assistance to, other developing countries, the very existence of OPEC might be at stake.

Clearly, bilaterial aid and charity alone are no longer sufficient and, in this respect, the proposed Agency will certainly represent a substantial improvement. But in order to appreciate the value of the Algerian–Venezuelan proposal for a new Agency, we need to consider briefly the serious failures and inadequacies of the present system of international cooperation. It is, indeed, in response to these shortcomings that both the philosophy of the Agency and its proposed activities have been elaborated.

The failures of the present international framework of financial cooperation

It is generally admitted today that the Bretton Woods Agreement reflected the financial and monetary concerns of developed industrial countries. The International Monetary Fund system instituted at Bretton Woods was, in both its philosophy and institutions, very much a product of the immediate post-war period. It was designed to operate concurrently with, chiefly, an international arrangement by which funds for the reconstruction of the devastated economies in the developed countries could be secured. Moreover, by sharply separating questions of employment, trade and incomes from monetary and financial questions, even the financial mechanisms of the IMF turned out to be solely geared to the problems of the developed countries. In short, the Bretton Woods Agreement resulted in totally overlooking the fundamental disequilibrium between developed and developing countries.

Today, despite the collapse of the Bretton Woods exchange rate system in 1971 and the emergence of the 'dollar system', the philosophy of the Bretton Woods Agreement and their underlying view of the realities of the world economic conditions continue to shape the character of the international monetary system.

The following features of the Bretton Woods monetary system should be noted:

(i) *The sharp distinction drawn between short-term imbalances and long-term ones related to development problems*

It was thought that short-term deficits could be offset either through cyclical factors or by means of appropriate economic measures, the international community being expected to provide financial help in overcoming these temporary deficits. As for long-term deficits, it was the International Bank for Reconstruction and Development (IBRD) which was supposed to find the necessary funds for investment projects.

(ii) *The absence of any agreement on questions relating to incomes and employment*

These questions were supposed to be dealt with indirectly by the International Trade Organization (ITO). However, the ITO never came into existence, thus leaving balance of payment problems arising specifically from weak development fundamentally unresolved.

(iii) *The vague character of any measures for compulsory adjustment*

No provisions existed for identifying countries which should be made to adjust their exchange rates. This resulted in imbalances in the system because countries with a surplus could not be compelled to adjust their rates, and asset settlement in the US was not effective. However, post-war experience shows that full employment in the economics of developed countries could not be maintained in the face of sustained imbalances of payments. This clearly suggests that under an adequate international monetary system, there should exist provisions for adjusting structural imbalances at high levels of employment.

The three features listed above show why countries with reserve currencies enjoy a privileged position under the existing international monetary system. These countries might delay or even avoid adjustment by availing themselves of the reserves held in their currencies. However, this kind of partial approach (using classical demand management techniques) is not suitable for structural or externally caused deficits. Because these deficits are directly affected by the trade and economic policies of other countries and, more generally, by the overall pattern of international adjustments, the terms of the IMF are ill-adapted and of no relevance to them. (Access to IMF resources is conditional upon carrying out deflationary policies and exchange rate adjustments.)

Procedures for adjustment should therefore be more discriminate, taking into account the structural imbalances in the world economy, particularly as regards the developing countries. The fundamental lack of equilibrium between developed and developing countries makes it impossible to apply general rules for adjustment, and, in this respect, experience suggests that a hard-and-fast distinction between short-term and long-term deficits is inappropriate.

Moreover, on the tacit assumption that imbalances are due to economic mismanagement, there have been attempts to achieve short-term stability by concentrating on balancing payments independently of any requirements for long-term growth. But this assumption has seldom proved true, and, here again, experience shows that the severe deflationary measures imposed on many developing economies have resulted in very low levels of income, employment and resource utilization.

It would thus appear that the IMF needs to develop special policy tools for dealing with problems which, although falling under the general heading of payment deficits, are really diverse in nature. Instead of treating all imbalances as if they were of a temporary nature, the system should include provision specifically tailored for the needs of the developing countries.

Existing adjustment mechanisms, which usually correct imbalances asymmetrically at the expense of the growth rate of countries in deficit, should therefore be abandoned.

In recent years, funds for adjustment have come from the capital markets of private investors, so that countries judged to be credit-worthy were able to secure liquid funds, even if problems of external debt-financing and servicing were exacerbated as a result. The magnitude of these problems can be gauged if one remembers that, in the period between 1974 and 1979, developing countries other than oil-producers registered a cumulative current account deficit amounting to $195 billion, whilst their commercial debt liability increased by more than $150 billion. Needless to say, this situation arose because the major developed countries, by reducing imports and securing better terms of trade, had transferred their deficits to the developing countries, including OPEC countries. However, since poorer developing countries have little or no ability to borrow on the international market on commercial terms, or can do so only at high cost, they must look outside the private capital markets. Thus, many of them have been compelled to use the IMF, thereby having to bear most of the burden of the deflation needed for adjustment. Peru, Sudan and Egypt are cases in point. On the whole, however, the majority of these poor nations prefer to resort to full domestic deflation rather than enter into a standby agreement with the IMF, whose terms disregard the sovereign right of states to determine their own road to development and evolve their own social and economic models. Such has been the choice of Tanzania and Jamaica. Clearly, in a world where deficits are badly affecting the world economy, IMF resources have never been so important.

This situation is likely to continue as long as it is not realized that developing countries are not responsible for the greatest part of their deficits. These deficits are in fact due to factors such as fluctuating or low export prices, low demand for imports, high rates of inflation worldwide, increasingly unfavourable terms of trade and high interest rates. Such factors must be taken into account whenever any attempt is made at determining how much access Third World countries should have to the higher credit blocks of the IMF.

One of the asymmetrical features of the Bretton Woods system has been the existence of structural imbalances of payments among the major developed economies, as well as, since 1974, the financial surpluses of the oil-exporting countries. In the case of industrialized countries, payments surpluses are due to long-run factors, such as a lead in areas of essential technology exports, well-established market networks and economies of scale. In contrast, surpluses in oil-exporting countries are temporary phenomena; they are due to a world demand for oil which far exceeds the revenue required by these countries. This high demand for oil reflects consumption and production patterns based on levels of oil prices below those of alternative energy sources − a price structure which is due, it hardly bears mentioning, to the pricing policies adopted by the oil companies from the early forties until 1978.

In 1973/4 a large number of Western studies estimated that, by 1980, oil assets would amount to a staggering $600 to $800 billion. This prediction, however, turned out to be far from accurate: from 1975 until the middle of 1979, official OPEC oil prices declined in real terms, and it was not until the end of 1979 that this tendency was reversed by OPEC, bringing the real price level back to the 1974 level. This goes to show that, although some OPEC countries did accumulate financial surpluses, these surpluses never reached the very high levels predicted in 1973/4 by Western media. In March 1980 surpluses resulting from oil assets did not amount to more than $180 billion. On the other hand, Euro-currencies amounted to $1,200 billion (estimated on the basis of foreign currency liabilities and claims by major European banks operating in the Bahamas, Bahrein, Cayman Islands, Panama, Canada, Japan, Hong Kong and Singapore). This clearly shows that OPEC surpluses still represent a small proportion of global liquid assets. Moreover, the expected size of future OPEC surpluses could well be smaller. According to an OPEC forecast published in June 1980, exports of high technology services by industrial countries have offset growing interest earnings on the current account surplus accumulated by OPEC, while the drop in the volume of oil exports due to higher prices and slow OECD activity is expected to actually reduce the surplus in 1981. Nevertheless, since the economic requirements and energy needs of the eighties seem to preclude any sharp drop in the level of real oil prices similar to that of 1973–9, we should expect OPEC surpluses to remain quite substantial. In any case, for the time being, OPEC surpluses have been estimated at $110–15 billion for 1980, and at $100 billion for 1982.

It is thus clear that the existing international Monetary System has failed in two respects. First, it was unable to provide means for bringing within its province at least part of the combined surpluses of developed countries and OPEC countries, and secondly, it was unable to integrate these financial claims within the structure of world liquid assets. In the case of OPEC surpluses for instance, the IMF was unable to find investment revenues for them. In fact, representatives from the developed countries refused at the CIEC Paris Conference to give special consideration to OPEC surplus assets, despite the fact that such surplus assets represent a real sacrifice on the part of these developing countries, who have to produce more oil than they need in order to satisfy world-wide economic requirements.

More important still is the fact that since November 1980 the US Government has frozen the public assets of Iran. Again, there was no regular IMF mechanism by which to channel OPEC surpluses towards investment venues, nor have any means been devised to integrate these surpluses into the central supply of funds.

Here it should be stressed that the oil facility of 1974 was a temporary measure designed to alleviate the payments problems of the developed countries, as was the Supplementary Financial Facility (SFF) created in 1979 — a facility run on commercial terms and carrying strict lending conditions. This meant that the only alternative left for oil-exporting countries was to invest the bulk of their surplus funds in the private financial markets, which then recycled them and channelled them to deficit countries able to satisfy their credit-worthiness standards. As to most other developing countries, it was left to the Official Development Assistance (ODA) to assist them in overcoming their tragic problems.

The cost of using the banks as intermediaries has undoubtedly been very high, whilst the absence of adequate financial channels continues to prevent any substantial recycling of oil surpluses to developing countries — notwithstanding what these countries receive by way of generous aid transfers from oil assets. However, since the volume of trade between OPEC and the industrial countries is much greater than with the developing countries, it is more profitable for OPEC to hold its financial claims against the industrial countries. It is thus clear that, in the absence of a reformed IMF system that could provide a stable pool of funds recyclable through banking processes under international collective responsibility, an alternative, Third World solution must be sought.

OPEC and the establishment of a new framework for financial and economic cooperation: the new OPEC Development Agency

The flaws in the existing system of international cooperation affect adversely not only developing countries, but OPEC countries as well. These countries suffer from an erosion in the value of their financial assets, and from rising import prices — a factor which pushes up the cost of the development programmes they must pursue in order to secure revenues once oil supplies have been exhausted. It is for this reason that OPEC countries have taken a lead in pressing for the new international economic order called for by the special UN General Assembly in 1974-5. One point emphasized there by oil-exporting countries with surplus problems was the need to restructure international financial institutions and monetary mechanisms. Similarly, at the fifth UNCTAD session at Manila, it was reaffirmed that the international monetary system should provide, among other things, 'ways and means of maintaining the real value of the financial assets of developing countries by preventing their erosion through inflation and exchange depreciation' (Resolution 128(v) — international monetary reform paragraph (D)).

It is thus clear that a fundamental aspect of any reform of the world monetary and financial order must be the strengthening of monetary and financial cooperation among developing countries.

In fact, the Arusha programme for collective self-reliance stated precisely that 'economic cooperation among developing countries is a basic component of the efforts towards the establishment of the new international economic order' (NIEO, item 18, page 96, paragraph b).

Besides many recommendations dealing with arrangements for multilateral payments and the creation of an export credit guarantee facility, the programme for collective self-reliance recommended that the UNCTAD secretariat submit a report on the feasibility of establishing a bank for developing countries (paragraph 17 (iii)). Also, in September 1979 at Belgrade, a meeting of ministers from the Group of Seventy-seven reaffirmed the importance of monetary and financial cooperation among developing countries, stressing that cooperation is an integral part of any change in the world monetary and financial order. The same meeting added that the Group of Twenty will seek ways and means to contribute to the elaboration of specific mechanisms through which monetary and financial cooperation among developing countries could be implemented, both in the light of the OECD programmes and on the basis of its own initiatives (Blue Books). All these recommendations paved the way for the Algerian–Venezuelan proposal entitled 'Joint Proposal by the Algerian and Venezuelan Delegations on the Need for Additional Financial Cooperation Between OPEC Member Countries and Other Developing Countries'; this proposal was submitted to the ministerial conference of OPEC held in Caracas in December 1979.

But there were earlier moves along these lines. For instance, as early as the initial adjustment of oil prices in late 1973, perhaps even earlier, OPEC member countries perceived the need for a multilateral effort of international cooperation extended on a bilateral basis by the member countries to the other developing countries. The 1975 conference of sovereigns and heads of state which took place in Algiers gave concrete content to the need for such an institution by creating the OPEC Special Fund. This it did with a view to alleviating the balance of payments problems of other developing countries and helping them in their process of development.

The creation of this OPEC Special Fund implied recognition by OPEC of the structural character of underdevelopment in the developing countries. This underdevelopment is due to the political and economic domination to which all developing countries (including OPEC) are subjected under the present world economic system, a situation which calls for appropriate remedial measures by the developed nations to eradicate underdevelopment from the world. However, developed countries have so far failed to adopt any such measures. This is clearly illustrated in the past few years by the drop in the real value of ODA grants, contrary to stated objectives.

In the face of this, and despite the fact that they are in no way responsible for the economic conditions of developing nations, OPEC countries have played an increasingly important role in providing support for these nations — thus recognizing the need for greater international solidarity amongst the countries of the Third World. This type of action is necessary because, as we have seen, it is the control exercised by a small number of developed countries over the multilateral financial institutions which stands in the way of satisfying the needs of the developing countries. Meanwhile, the request of these countries for better adapted adjustment procedures and for the use of different criteria in assessing and reforming the terms of the IMF goes unheeded.

In view of the pressing nature of the problems faced by developing countries which do not produce oil, and because of OPEC's solidarity with these countries, OPEC has decided to act alone. In doing so, however, OPEC countries wish to stress that they are in no way responsible for the economic problems of the developing countries, and that they have no intention of permanently replacing the developed countries as providers of aid to the Third World. The financial measures included in the proposal should thus be understood in the context of a more general scheme of financial cooperation with the developing countries, as outlined in the Arusha Programme or the Blue Books.

Nor should it be thought that this OPEC effort is meant to relieve the industrial countries from having to provide assistance grants commensurate with the extent of the responsibility they bear for the problems of structural under-development in the Third World. In this context, the authors of the proposal did recognize that the OPEC Special Fund has achieved the limited objectives it was given. Today, however, the size of this fund and its legal status are no longer adequate for providing the types of grants and the amounts of payments needed to assist other developing countries.

The importance of multilateral financial cooperation between OPEC and other countries becomes even more obvious if one looks at international developments since 1974.

For instance, one point which transpired from the Manila Conference is that it is becoming increasingly difficult for developing countries (including OPEC) to maintain a united front in various international forums. This is no doubt essentially due to the worsening economic situation of many Third World countries, who have suffered from the economic monetary and commercial policies of the developed countries (inflation, deflation, debt and import barriers) as well as from the unjust structure of international economic relations. This structure clearly condemns the Third World to a future of permanent underdevelopment unless adequate counter-measures are adopted.

Moreover, the most recent increase in oil prices (following the sharp drop in crude oil prices between 1974 and 1979) has aggravated the external situation of some developing countries, despite the fact that this increase can only have *a one-time impact*, unlike the impact of the export prices of industrial countries and of debt servicing.

It is thus morally incumbent upon OPEC countries to act in solidarity with other developing countries. The way to do this is for OPEC countries to use their financial and economic strength in order to spearhead those needed changes in the structure of the international economic system. OPEC resources could thus help create a strong momentum for building up self-reliance in Third World countries, the consequence of which would be to introduce important changes in the present division of labour. Uncompetitive types of exports produced in the developing countries would thus have to be gradually abandoned, particularly in cases where the comparative long-term advantage lies with these countries. This, indeed, is the course mapped out by the Declaration and Action Programme at Lima, but which, so far, developing countries have been reluctant to take.

A further consideration is that the necessary dialogue with the North will be more successful if the solidarity of all developing countries is already reinforced and protected by a commitment of OPEC countries to an adequate policy. Such a policy should include two main components: (i) it should have adequate provisions and institutions designed specifically for other developing countries, and (ii) it should aim at securing from the industrial countries a more concrete commitment to provide financial assistance to the developing economies. The policy should also have two complementary objectives: first, an OPEC undertaking to increase its financial aid to other developed countries in order to alleviate their immediate economic problems, and secondly, the establishment of a more permanent mechanism of financial cooperation that can help these countries in their process of development.

According to the authors of the proposal, these two types of help should always aim at making the recipient countries *more self-reliant* and *less vulnerable*. In the field of energy, for instance, the purpose of OPEC assistance should be to facilitate the Third World transition towards an era of oil prices that truly reflect the cost of alternative energy sources — although in no case should this assistance attempt to shield the recipient countries from the desirable and unavoidable trend of rising energy prices. The priorities set forth by the UN concerning the distribution of aid (e.g. top priority to the least developed, most seriously affected, countries) should be adhered to, although all countries will be eligible for OPEC aid, relative to their respective energy resources and economic conditions. The authors of the proposal also agreed that the conditions of financing should be *suited to the general economic situation of each country, its degree of dependency on imported energy and the situation of its balance of payments*. As for developing countries who have access to the private capital market, they should be able to receive OPEC aid as soon as the terms imposed by the IMF for financing their deficits begin to force them to abandon their priorities and the particular road to development their peoples have chosen through their legitimate representatives. The authors of the proposal also agreed that, although existing bilateral assistance mechanisms between OPEC member countries are of great importance, a multilateral *OPEC arrangement* for international financial cooperation could be a much more effective measure for achieving the long-term objectives of Third World countries, including those of OPEC.

As to long-term OPEC objectives, they saw these as necessitating the creation of an Agency backed by OPEC countries and possessing its own international legal status.

This decision to create an Agency rather than a bank was

reached after lengthy discussions. It was thought that an agency would be more compatible with the motives of OPEC assistance, since it could simultaneously fill the two roles of providing traditional assistance (like the ODA) and other types of financing more similar to the usual banking type. Moreover, in practical terms, this agency could be created by modifying the OPEC Special Fund.

The most important aspect of this Agency would be its ability to strengthen the solidarity of OPEC countries and other developing countries by *pooling their credit capacities* for the benefit of all developing countries. As to the principal function of this Agency, it would be to provide funds for general development projects — particularly those projects likely to promote trade amongst developing countries and lessen their dependence on imported energy.

With such an agency, not only could the credit capacity of OPEC be used to provide substantially greater assistance to developing countries, but the latter will also be given the opportunity to penetrate the sphere of international finance — a sphere hitherto closed to all but the industrial countries. Moreover, the banking side of the Agency would constitute a nucleus around which payments could be pooled and a Third World capital market organized. Later, the possibility should be considered of setting up a real mechanism for recycling all Third World surpluses (not just those resulting from oil exports).

An initial authorized capital fund of $20 billion has been proposed for the Agency. This amount could be increased from time to time. Share subscriptions would be composed of a 50 per cent cash part and a 50 per cent callable part, so that the Agency could start its operations with a $5 billion cash deposit (viz. the cash part of a $10 billion subscription representing half the total initial authorized capital).

The Agency would function as an intergovernmental institution organized along the lines of similar multinational institutions for financing development projects. It would issue securities — such as bonds — on the international financial markets, offering adequate rates of return and protection against inflation. An equitable and efficient recycling mechanism would thus come into effect, thereby securing an optimal diversification of assets for the surplus countries and a permanent larger net share of resources for the developing countries.

Furthermore, through the Agency, it would be possible to use the large credit capacity of OPEC countries as a guarantee against loans from the industrial countries, particularly in the case of developing countries with no access to private capital markets. Other measures could also be adopted to enable the lesser developed countries to tap the resources of commercial banks throughout the world. Further still, specific interest rate subsidies schemes could be devised. In short, it would be possible to introduce a wide variety of loan guarantee plans within the framework of the Agency.

As to the launching of the Agency, the proposal firmly recommends that it should be the founding members of the Agency who should initially purchase a large proportion of its securities so as to create a market for them and help establish confidence in the Agency.

The proposal also stresses that the loans by the Agency should be granted on the basis of a thorough financial and economic analysis of the relevant development project, with a view to securing adequate interest earnings and repayment of the loan. This policy is necessary because the Agency will be endowed with very large funds of which 50 per cent is paid-in, cost-free capital which could be lent over longer periods of time and at a lower interest rate than on the international financial market. This policy would also enable the Agency to have a special section for concessional loans to the least developed countries and, more generally, to take into account a country's particular situation in setting out the terms of the loans.

Listed below are some of the activities which the Agency will be expected to engage in:

1 Providing funds at favourable terms for social and economic programmes which are given priority by the recipient country. Such programmes would include the development of renewable and non-renewable energy sources.

2 Financing projects likely to bring developing countries closer together, thus increasing their collective self-reliance.

3 Financing projects intended to upgrade the value of raw materials produced by the developing countries.

4 Underwriting export credit transactions amongst developing countries, especially in the area of energy.

5 Financing commercial operations by the developing countries at the prevailing market rate.

6 Financing balance of payments deficits and underwriting loans obtained on financial markets by developing countries.

7 Promoting projects which use the domestic production capacity and service of the developing countries. It should be noted in this respect that specially adapted terms will be given to those countries which are worst affected or least developed.

Note finally that the procedure for obtaining loans and guarantees should be expeditious and flexible, unlike the current practice of existing international financial institutions.

The Agency should start operating in January 1981, following its creation at the meeting of OPEC sovereigns and heads of state.

The criteria and objectives listed above are not exhaustive; they are only examples of what the Agency could do in order to strengthen both cooperation and self-reliance in the Third World.

Conclusion

With the implementation of this project, billions of dollars could be recycled in the coming years amongst developing countries, thus securing for them greater self-reliance. Moreover, it is interesting to note that at the last annual meeting (September 1980) of the World Bank, the then president, Mr McNamara, spoke of the need to create a new institution for funding energy projects, a suggestion which came only months after the creation by the World Bank of a Credit Fund for Structural Adjustment, and after the Brandt Commission's public call for a Development Fund with participation by OPEC. This goes to show that there is nothing

incongruous about the Algerian–Venezuelan proposal: undoubtedly, its existence alone has already prompted the
re-emergence of projects which the so-called Group of
Twenty-four has been trying to implement for years.

At a time when the demand for greater cooperation
among the countries of the South is growing, and the first
round of general negotiations has failed, the developing
world should, more than ever before, try to secure suitable
means to determine its own destiny. For this purpose,
existing surpluses could be drawn upon to fund many projects, be it the exploitation of new or traditional energy
sources, the promotion and distribution of local technology,
or the exchange of skilled labour between different countries. Such an exchange is already taking place between
some Eastern countries and some Gulf states.

Clearly, there is no shortage of opportunities. What is
needed is a political commitment, and for OPEC to assume
its responsibilities.

3 THE 'MASSIVE TRANSFER' OF RESOURCES TO DEVELOPING COUNTRIES

Dr Lal Jayawardena*

'Massive transfer' may be defined as substantial transfers that take place under official auspices but outside of the government budget of developed donor countries, and which in addition can be distinguished from private foreign investment in developing countries. The concern expressed here with 'massive transfer' is based upon the circumstance that there appears to be a number of constraints today which affect other categories of flows, that are not readily amenable to policy action.

For instance, the target for official development assistance of 0.7 per cent is observed more in the breach than in the observance, and on any normal reckoning of the potential for progress in this area, today's 0.3 per cent or thereabouts cannot be expected to reach beyond 0.35 or 0.37 per cent.

Private foreign investment, on the other hand, responds to definable policies, both on the side of the investing country and of the host country. Its precise evolution in response to any set of policies is not easily predictable. It is for these reasons that attention has increasingly centred on other ways of getting resources transferred to developing countries; and the main conclusion of this chapter is that if the Third World is in present circumstances to play the role of an 'Engine of Growth' in the world economy, then an annual transfer outside these categories of flows of the order of $25 to $50 billion appears to be called for.

President Castro, speaking on behalf of the Non-Aligned Group of Nations, assessed the need of these countries as

* Dr Lal Jayawardena is Ambassador of Sri Lanka to Belgium, Netherlands and Luxembourg and to the European Community.

$300 billion for the decade of the 1980s. These orders of magnitude have to be contrasted with present ODA levels of about $20 billion. In other words, the proposal seeks to add, internationally, as much to transfer as conventionally takes place through ODA, the channel that governments directly control through their budgets.

Against this brief background, the following four principal themes are being developed.

The first is to attempt to summarize the nature of the current international consensus on what can be termed 'massive resource transfer'. The second is to discuss the current global macro-economic situation and its relationship to any programme of transfer. The third is to try to construct a bridge between the current world economic situation and a concrete proposal for massive transfer — namely, a set of transitional steps towards a more durable scheme. And, fourthly, to try to sketch the outline of such a concrete proposal for 'massive transfer'.

The international consensus on 'massive transfer'

Of these four themes, the easiest to cover is the nature of the current consensus on this whole question. For this we have, paradoxically enough, two resolutions in the UNCTAD[1] discussion that dealt with money and finance in March 1980. Both these resolutions are significant because they indicate the wide-ranging territory that the notion of 'massive transfer' covers both substantively and politically. In some respects, one can argue that there was more of a consensus on this whole question of 'massive transfer' than might appear at first sight to have been the case. The UNCTAD Consensus Resolution on 'Massive Transfer', the first incidentally to use that specific term, came up with two areas of political agreement which represent a step forward. The first is the recognition for the first time that 'massive transfers' were an 'indispensable factor' for promoting the development of developing countries and 'could help stimulate global economic activity particularly in a medium- to long-term perspective'.[2]

The second major area of political agreement was the

spelling out of criteria which any concrete proposal for giving effect to 'massive transfers' ought to conform to. There were five criteria in all. The first quite obviously was that any proposal ought to 'be compatible with the development priorities of developing countries'. The second was that it should pay special attention to those developing countries which depend 'primarily on concessional funds for external financing'. The third, which is at the heart of any 'massive transfer' proposal, is that the amounts are to 'be largely raised in international financial markets' and do not have therefore to burden the budgets of developed countries. Fourthly, there was the recognition of the need to 'take into account the possibility of interest subsidy mechanisms' as a way of reconciling the two immediately preceding criteria with one another. The final criterion concerns the uses to which these transfers will be put; these would be 'for project development and execution and programme financing purposes'. Altogether the resolution represented something of a minor triumph for the Group of Seventy-seven in that the criteria embodied their thinking as expressed in the Arusha Programme of Action. This was that 'the mechanism' for massive transfer 'would analytically imply the raising under the collective guarantee of the international community of monies in international capital markets and their disbursement to developing countries over a long term period, with an interest subsidy element as appropriate, in the form of both project and programme lending for structural change'.[3]

Now this much of the consensus was achieved in what is conventionally called the area of 'financial issues'. The UNCTAD Negotiating Group that considered these issues dealt also with what are conventionally called 'monetary issues' as distinct from financial issues. In that area too there was endorsement of a proposal which for analytical purposes is not very easy to separate out from the notion of 'massive transfer'.

While the generality of IMF facilities are of a 3 to 5 year duration, there has in recent years been established an 'extended facility' where money is given to countries under fairly tight conditions for up to eight years, and most recently up to ten years. The concern expressed in UNCTAD was that periods even as long as this were too short given the structural problems of developing countries so that there was a need to get additional resources routed through the IMF for this range of purposes. Analytically, however, what was called 'massive transfer' within the category of 'financial issues' and the 'longer-term financing facility' within the IMF and hence falling within the category of 'monetary issues' deal with precisely the same sort of problem and come economically to the same thing.

Global macro-economic management, recycling and massive transfer: history and prospects

It is perhaps convenient to begin with the very obvious and tautological proposition that characterizes the international accounts of any global trading system at the end of any accounting year. This is that in statistical terms the algebraic sum of the balance of payments surpluses and deficits on current account of countries within the system come to zero. In other words, in so far as there are current account surpluses such as those run by OPEC today or by major developed economies such as Japan, Germany and Switzerland, there are counterpart deficits *that will have been financed* that exactly equal the surpluses that are run. This equality obtains logically *ex post* as part of any year's accounting; it, in fact, only indicates that the surpluses will have been *on lent* by some combination or other of mechanisms to the countries whose deficits will have been financed, some deficit developing and other developed countries, and further that these countries will have been willing to *accept* these deficits and the associated terms of financing. In other words, this accounting identity reflects the availability of acceptable mechanisms for on-lending surpluses to deficit countries.

Now these surpluses change *over time* through really two routes. To the extent to which countries have had surplus positions in the past can expand their imports in the subsequent period, these surpluses obviously would diminish reducing the counterpart deficits and releasing the strain on financing mechanisms that had previously coped. This obviously is one route through which surpluses can be diminished and deficits reduced.

The other route, of course, is by a cumulative decline in economic activity within the system as a whole, so that all round there is a curtailment of trade affecting both exports and imports. The system will eventually settle at whatever level is determined by the capacity and acceptability of the mechanisms that are *in fact* used to recycle or on-lend these surpluses to deficit countries. In other words, three mechanisms would contribute to change over time in surplus situations, an expansion of imports by surplus countries, acceptable ways of on-lending surpluses to deficit countries and finally a decline in economic activity to whatever level is permitted by these two mechanisms.

What happened in the seventies was that all these three mechanisms had been working in the global economy. Since 1973 there was the emergence of substantial OPEC surpluses which were extinguished in fact rather more rapidly than most people expected by increased imports. In 1973 the total OPEC surplus was about $5 billion. It went up in subsequent years to between $35 and $40 billion, and then in 1978 it was back to $5 million, though in 1979 it increased rather sharply to reflect the oil-price increases of that year. The decline, however, was to some extent the result of a very rapid expansion in the imports of OPEC countries by nearly 60 per cent in the seventies.

The second route that was taken was the rapid expansion in bank lending to developing countries. It is now customary to acknowledge that the banking system of the world performed much better in the seventies than anyone was at that time prepared to give it credit for.

What basically happened was that OPEC surpluses were placed in banks as short-term deposits and banks, not finding a demand for funds in the developed world, found one way or another of channelling them to the developing countries. As a result, the non-OPEC developing countries' borrowings increased substantially and the facts indicate an increase from something like $35 billion in 1974 to $150 billion in 1979. The net external financing of balance of payments

deficits of developing countries by the banking system today
is of the order of two-thirds the total compared with one-
third in 1974; there has been an enormous shift in the
composition of debt of developing countries from conventional official development assistance to private debt contracted from banks. The other relevant fact, of course, is that the
IMF played a very small part indeed in all of this financing;
it accounted for only about 3 per cent of the financing of
developing countries' balance of payments deficits over the
period since 1974.

The problem of recycling then was accomplished by bank
lending and the 'load' on this particular mechanism was
eased by increased imports of the OPEC countries themselves. To the extent to which both mechanisms did not
work sufficiently well, what occurred inevitably was a
contraction of global economic activity. This point is important to emphasize. If one thinks of the world economy as
growing at some warranted rate of growth – a rate high
enough to fully employ presently unutilized capacities
within the system – then this would have generated significantly larger balance of payments surpluses on current
account and correspondingly larger deficits requiring to be
financed. The fact that the global economy has slumped to
the levels it has merely indicates that the mechanisms for
financing deficits have not worked as effectively as they
might have. The world economy has in fact tended to settle
down to the level determined by whatever mechanisms
were available to on-lend surpluses in order to keep trade
and activity going.

These general points are illustrated rather nicely by one
or two citations from available EEC documents. The first
of these is from the Community's *Annual Economic Review
1978–9* and is as follows:

The present equilibrium of the world economy, depends
to a considerable degree on a continuing flow of private
lending to the non oil producing developing countries
(and to the Soviet Union and Eastern Europe) on a scale
unheard of before 1974, *and would be called into question
by any impediment to that flow.* This flow of lending is

also of interest in the Community context — because a significant proportion of the loans have been made by banks resident in the EEC.[4]

The second is from a work entitled *Europe and the Third World: A Study on Interdependence* which indicates the pivotal role of the Third World in sustaining developed country export demand.

In fact, the Third World is the Community's principal customer and in 1977 37.6% of our exports went to developing countries compared with 12.5% to the United States and 9% to the Eastern State trading countries. Only our exports to the North European countries reach comparable figures, accounting for 22% of our total exports.

The most dynamic export markets within the developing countries are the OPEC countries. This is mainly due to the increase in oil prices and the enormous transfer of income ensuing therefrom. Since 1973, the share of exports to OPEC countries has more than doubled, from 8.2% in 1973 to 18.1% of total exports in 1977.

Even the non-oil producing developing countries present more reliable and dynamic outlets than the industrialized countries. Had the developing countries followed the example of the industrialized countries after 1973, by cutting back both their growth and imports to adjust to the oil price increases, the recession in the industrialized countries would have been far more serious. The figures for 1975, when our economies reached their lowest point, are particularly striking. While Community exports to the United States fell by 17% (in EUA terms) and those to the EFTA countries by 3.3%, our exports to the developing countries increased by 25%, those to the ACP countries alone by 33%.[5]

The point being emphasized here is that it was the recycling process that made it possible for demand to be maintained during a very difficult period and for the level of world economic activity to have been sustained.

It is against this background of a relatively successful

adjustment to the problem of the 1970s that one confronts an outlook for the 1980s which does not, in the view of many, leave room for much complacency. There are several aspects to this somewhat sombre note on which the decade of the 1980s begins. In the first place, the result of current market developments has been, of course, the very large OPEC surplus that is expected for 1980. Present projections suggest a magnitude of a $100 billion for this surplus this year, which is larger than any previous figure; an overall developed country deficit of $30 billion, and a non-oil-developing country deficit, all on current account of $73 billion.[6]

Now this itself is not new or worrying, but what has given cause for concern is the probable persistence of a surplus situation of this kind until the middle 1980s. The first to voice their concern over this have been key private banking sources, and this itself is of significance. The first long-term projections of surpluses of OPEC have come from the Chairman of the Board of West Deutsche Landesbank, Dr Seipp, on 10 January, and the Senior Vice-President of Morgan Guaranty, Rimmer de Vries, a month earlier. Dr Seipp's forecast[7] is of a cumulative surplus for OPEC of $400 billion between 1979 and 1983, as compared with $160 billion, cumulatively, during 1974 to 197 . De Vries' estimates are of the same order of magnitude.[8] These forecasts imply that the net external assets of the OPEC countries will grow correspondingly over this period.

The third fact, apart from the expected persistence of surpluses, is the very real fear now being voiced by private banks that they cannot now cope with the recycling problem. These fears were also expressed in the post-1973 period and they were somehow overcome as the banking system proved adequate to the task of recycling. But this very success in the eyes of many who have looked at the issue currently implies that the difficulties this time are of a vastly greater degree.

Reuters have, as recently as 25 January 1980, judged 'the balance of opinion of Bankers and Bank economists around the world questioned by Reuter correspondents' as being that 'the world's commercial banking system will be *unable* to recycle the enormous increase in revenue the Oil Producing Countries are set to receive *without the help of such international financial organisations as the IMF or of individual governments*.[9] Similarly, Dr Seipp feels categorically able to say that 'Bankers are not in a position to solve on their own the problem in its presently known magnitudes'.[10]

There are currently two reasons for this concern. In the first place, the Banks this time round are called upon to lend to countries that have already borrowed from them previously; they are naturally cautious, therefore, about overextending their exposure to particular countries. So far as the US is concerned, something like 45 per cent of total US claims on foreign countries, other than the Group of Ten and Switzerland, are focused now on only seven developing countries — Argentina, Brazil, Korea, Mexico, the Philippines, Taiwan and Venezuela.[11] Altogether, six non-OPEC developing countries — this same list, in fact, minus Venezuela and Taiwan, with the addition of Peru — had at the end of 1977 outstanding debts from banks of $62 billion and accounted for three-quarters of all Euromarket borrowing by developing countries.[12] Early in 1980 some of these countries themselves, conscious of their high debt service ratios, began to cut back on their borrowing in Euromarkets.[13]

One result of this concern with the risks of overconcentration of lending, as far as US banks are concerned, has been a decline in the last two years or so of their rate of lending to developing countries as compared with the previous several years. Thus, a 31 per cent annual expansion of lending to developing countries between 1970 and 1976 declined to 13 per cent annually in the period.

The new element though in the current situation, which did not arise in the early 1970s, is a preoccupation by banks with the adequacy of their own capital. The banking system operates on rules about safe ratios between their own equity and their assets; these latter, of course, comprise their loans to countries and enterprises which, in turn, are determined by the deposits placed with them by owners of surplus funds. Concern over the adequacy of capital to assets ratios translates itself fairly readily into a reluctance to receive additional OPEC deposits and the signs are increasingly evident. Thus, in the case of US money centre banks the capital to assets ratio has declined from 4.5 per cent in 1972 to 3.5 per cent in September 1979.[14] Indeed, in the case of certain continental banks this decline has proceeded to the point where they have begun actively to discourage OPEC countries from depositing monies with them, by quoting depositors' rates below the going inter-bank rate. The problem of adequacy of capital has resulted in particular cases, such as the Commerzbank and Bayerische Vereinsbank, from the fact of their having replenished their equity recently in the market, and the difficulty they have as a result of going again to the market to raise additional equity.[15] The concern then with the adequacy of capital is the new element in the current situation.

The third factor that makes for a worrying outlook for the 1980s is that the absorptive capacity of OPEC – their capacity rapidly to expand their imports – appears to be much less now than in the 1970s. There are a variety of reasons for this. There is certainly room for suspicion that the lessons that have arisen out of Iran's attempt to plunge headlong into rapid development programmes may have a bearing on the pace at which some of the more traditional OPEC countries decide to transform their societies. There is already evidence of a scaling down of ambitious development plans and overall import levels are bound to suffer in consequence.

Fourthly, an important element which moderated the recessionary impact during the 1970s appears now to be absent in so far as many of the developed countries which at that time pursued expansionary policies are now not doing so. This is especially true of the UK and Italy, where real and understandable concern with controlling inflation, has meant restrictionist domestic policies and a reversal of previous policies.

What has been said so far amounts to this – that those factors which moderated the situation overall in the 1970s are not now likely to prevail. Banks will not be able to recycle monies in the way they previously did. OPEC will not be importing at the previous pace; and other developed countries will not be providing an expansionary bias. On this scenario, therefore, one is left with the probability of a truly massive deflation in the absence of corrective policy action. This point is worth emphasizing since there is little room for policy manœuvre in improving OPEC absorptive capacities and abandoning restrictionist domestic policies elsewhere. Indeed, the only area of effective policy action would appear to be in an effective recycling of surpluses to countries in deficit in order to sustain global activity by buttressing the prevailing weakness of the banking system. The policy choices involved are only too clear. Either you have very little recycling and more deflation because of the difficulties of the banks, or better recycling and less deflation. There can be no question of better recycling *increasing* inflation. This is perhaps the important point to note in the context of the current concern with inflation in the world economy. I would, therefore, define 'better recycling' today as being equivalent to a 'massive transfer' of resources to developing countries under official auspices which involves shifting from the relatively short-term lending – previously practised by banks – to making available longer-term programme financing on concessionary terms for poorer developing countries as well as to the traditional run of middle-income developing country borrower.

I have been concerned, so far, with a deflation scenario. But long before you get to deflation you will probably have, again in the absence of policy action, massive exchange rate instability in advance of deflation which might, of course, escalate and prolong the deflation when it is launched. The crux of the problem is that the 1980 surplus of OPEC will have the effect of increasing OPEC holdings of foreign exchange in a single year by a very *large amount* in relation to their existing stock of foreign exchange. On past experience anything from 30 to 50 per cent of the OPEC surpluses of any one year are deposited in commercial banks. This means that banks will be called upon to receive a flow ranging from $30 to $50 billion in 1980 compared with the stock of $87 billion that OPEC had placed with them by the middle of 1979.

Quite apart from the question of the 'overload' this may impose upon the banking system, the underlying concern is with the capacity of the markets to handle a sudden increment in bank deposits in relation to the existing stock without causing undue exchange-rate instability, as OPEC depositors seek to diversify the composition of their reserve portfolios away from dollars to include other currencies such as Deutschmarks. The point is that while these amounts are small in relation to the balance sheets of banks overall, they are large enough, or appear to be large enough, to cause genuine concern within influential sections of the banking community about the threat of exchange rate instability.

Transitional steps towards a scheme for massive transfer

One is, therefore, confronted with two sets of problems; a deflationary problem over the medium term as well as an exchange rate instability problem in the very near term. Recently a variety of proposals have come up for consideration for dealing simultaneously with both problems. But what seems immediately most promising, as constituting a set of transitional arrangements, is the prospect of action involving central banks that could, in some sense, take the load off amounts that would normally have otherwise been deposited in commercial banks and cause the problems I have alluded to. If, for example, the large oil producers want to diversify their assets away from dollars into other currencies, the markets will accommodate that desire at the expense both of exchange rate instability and unwanted increments to the money supply of countries whose currencies are being preferred as reserve assets. On the other hand, the central banks concerned have, in principle, the capacity to handle both instability and money supply problems by arranging to accommodate asset preferences in a negotiated series of off-market transactions. One such negotiating sequence may proceed illustratively as follows: the Saudi Arabian Monetary Authority, say, would sell the dollars it would have received for its oil to the Bundes Bank in exchange for securities denominated in Deutschmarks, that is, in the German currency. These securities would represent secondary reserve assets for the Saudis whose terms, as regards interest rate, maturity, etc., would be negotiated at somewhat *below* market rates to reflect some sharing of the exchange risk being borne by the Germans in selling Deutschmark securities for dollars.

The circuit would be completed by the Bundes Bank investing the dollars so acquired in the US in dollar denominated bonds on terms negotiated *above* market rates, thus permitting the Bundes Bank to share some of the remaining exchange risk with the US. This type of negotiating sequence has a precedent in the two-year Roosa Bonds, negotiated in the middle 1960s, to relieve pressure on the US dollar.

Its principal innovative aspect at the present time is that this sequence can enable monies to be lent to developing countries as well; for the dollars which find a home in the US at the end of the negotiating circuit as described could be re-lent to developing countries on longer terms, within, of course, a framework of suitable terms and conditions for financing their deficits. Given the amounts requiring to be negotiated this year, this form of re-lending could well be the nucleus of a 'massive resource' transfer proposal. In principle, the same result can be achieved through a negotiated dollar substitution account within the IMF. Indeed, the urgency of such an arrangement has been stressed by the Witteveen Group of Thirty in a report intended as a contribution to its discussion within the IMF. Nevertheless, the Group of Thirty is obliged to conclude that 'granted the likely strength of the trend towards the diversification of currency reserves, and the time it will take to put a Substitution Account into place, it is desirable that more explicit discussion should develop among the central banks concerned as to the ways in which the legitimate preferences of all parties may be met'.[16]

One interim approach which might guide these discussions is termed by this Group 'the foreign currency substitution channel' and is tantamount to the negotiating sequence described above[17] with the difference that relending to developing countries is not explicitly considered.

The advantage of adopting this approach is that this probably represents the most immediate means available for converting what would otherwise be a crisis into an opportunity, and that rapid action is more *likely to result* once leading central banks become engaged in the process.

In the short-run, however, since the securities that will have to be negotiated among central banks are in the nature of secondary reserve assets, they are likely to be of a relatively short duration. There may not be much room for manœuvre initially, therefore, regarding the *maturity* for relending the amount to developing countries. Hence, the short-run plausibility of the suggestion that the IMF becomes the intermediary for channelling these funds to developing countries.

There is, however, an opportunity here which is within reach of governments as distinct from central banks (and which could be grasped by them almost *pari passu* with negotiations among central banks), which could have the effect of placing this relending on a genuinely longer-term basis for programme financing purposes. This opportunity consists simply of acting upon what is perhaps the key recommendation of the Brandt Commission, which it formulated as follows: [18]

> We have shown how the 1980's will inevitably see massive increases in the deficits and debts of the developing countries. Further studies are badly needed of the range of those debts and deficits by 1985 and of the resources — both private and public — potentially available to meet them. *But it is already apparent that special measures are needed. The industrialised and the oil-exporting countries should reach agreement on their respective additional roles and additional lending capacities, both directly by each and in the form of jointly shared guarantees.* Given the new sense of the interdependence affecting all parties, it is essential that these two groups of countries join forces to transform this potential crisis into a new opportunity for co-operation — in the common interest.

Quite clearly, the existence of a framework of *central bank* cooperation, which will have the effect of recycling OPEC surpluses off-market and through official (IMF) channels to developing countries, will facilitate the negotiation of these 'jointly shared guarantees' between *governments* which can alone place this lending on an adequately longer-term footing. Indeed, the likely persistence for several years ahead of OPEC surpluses is what warrants the establishment of a governmentally agreed framework for financing the counter-part deficits on an acceptable, and relatively long-term, basis. And whatever arrangements are worked out in the interim, whether at the level of central banks or of government could well be treated as transitional steps towards a new institution such as the World Development Fund proposed by the Brandt Commission designed to fill *inter alia* a widely acknowledged gap in longer-term programme lending between the IMF as presently structured and the World Bank. For 'jointly shared guarantees' can always be given permanent institutional form by their conversion into the *callable* as distinct from *paid-in* capital of an institution. Callable capital in this sense represents nothing more than a system of limited joint and several guarantees furnished by the member governments participating in the institution. An appropriate sequence might then be for the guarantee arrangements alone[19] to be set up among interested countries in the first instance to enable the raising of monies for longer term lending, including in this the proceeds of off-market reserve diversification mechanisms. At a later stage it would only require the determination of paid-in capital obligations to establish a new institution.

An institutional mechanism for 'massive transfer'

If these transitional arrangements are thought of as paving the way to a new financial institution then the case for this has to be satisfactorily made. It is to this fourth task that the rest of this chapter will be devoted. The main objective of this institution is to fill a long-identified 'gap' between the Bank and Fund.

The gap relates to the substantial longer term balance of payments support required by many countries to tide them over extended periods of economic adjustment to major changes in the international economic movement such as those of the past programme. During the 70s this gap has been filled largely by the rapid growth of private bank lending. However, aside from their short maturity structure and potential instability, commercial loans are frequently not available in adequate volume and on appropriate terms to a significant number of countries. The extended facility of the IMF launched in 1974 has helped to address this problem but there are strong indications that more needs to be done. The scope for new initiatives remains significant.[20]

So argues the World Bank's most recent *World Development Report*.

Perhaps the most convenient way to begin the task of formulating a proposal for institutional reform would be to go back to the previous history when Bretton Woods was negotiated. What was especially interesting in the discussion of that period was the disposition to believe that the institutional separation that eventually came to be made between the IMF and the World Bank was an artificial one. There was a very strong current of thinking in 1945 to the effect that the problems of the 'short-term' and the 'long-term' could not be compartmentalized — that what are conventionally called 'stabilization' programmes would require long-term loans. This was the substance of the testimony before the US House of Representatives Banking and Currency Committee in March 1945 of Randolph Burgess, then the President of the Banker's Association, in arguing

that the objectives of Bretton Woods would be carried out best if there were but one International Financial Organisation instead of two. We think that one organisation would carry out the objectives more efficiently in a more orderly way and more economically than two. The rules regarding international exchange restrictions, parties and other such questions can be worked out through a stabilisation department of this institution than if such questions were relegated to an institution which had no responsibility in respect to long-term loans. *Some stabilisation programmes will call for long term loans.*[21]

One has here, at the very beginning of the Bretton Woods discussion, the notion that an IMF standby is not a self-contained operation; that if an IMF standby is to work properly it ought to be married to longer-term loans and for which there is only at the moment a broadly *ad hoc* coordination mechanism available. Typically countries go first to the IMF for their standbys or programme financing where facilities do not extend beyond 10 years at most and then to the IBRD which in the ideal case superintends long-term project lending for upwards of 30 years either directly or as the coordinator of a consortium. The missing area of finance relates to longer-term programme lending for upwards of 15 years. The private banking system has typically operated within the maximum range of IMF maturities and not beyond.

Now an institution designed to fill this gap could be set up in a variety of ways. In a formal sense it can be set up along the lines of the World Bank with some amount, let us say, 10 per cent, of capital being paid in, and 90 per cent being callable capital which would not burden and need in fact never burden participating countries' budgets. The callable capital constitutes in effect a system of limited joint and several guarantees being furnished by members of the institution to enable it to go to the market place and borrow against this callable capital. It results only in a contingent liability for governments, limited in each case by the amount of callable capital, to honour the obligations of the institution in the very remote contingency of the institution being unable to service its debt.

It is evident that by the time an institution is fully negotiated the current opportunity could well be lost. But what the present emergency suggests is a three-phased operation which would proceed from emergency to more permanent arrangements. In the first phase, the central banks of the key governments could work together as previously outlined to implement an 'off-market' reserve diversification cum recycling mechanism, and then make available resources for an emergency programme for developing countries as well as, of course, sustaining global demand generally.

In the second phase, the governments of the cooperating central banks could give thought to implementing the Brandt Commission recommendation involving especially 'jointly shared guarantees'[22] between OPEC and developed countries concerning the financing of developing country deficits so as in effect to put phase one on an adequately longer-term footing. These guarantees would in effect correspond to the callable capital of any future institution and could indeed pave the way for one. This second phase could constitute the nucleus of an institution without the need to pay in any capital subscription at all, and avoiding the resultant drain on government's budgets though interest subsidy arrangements would need to be devised which can again be financed outside of government budgets as will presently be indicated.

The third stage, depending on how these two stages work, would encompass the detailed negotiations required for a fully fledged international institution to be born. The first two stages will, of course, mean that it would be countries which have an urgent stake in the current global economic situation that will have taken an initiative leading to something of a longer-term character. It would indeed be possible, and in some respects preferable, if emergency action, as in phase one, were to dovetail in phase two with arrangements for transforming the OPEC Special Fund into a Development Agency as contemplated by the governments of Algeria and Venezuela, for engaging *inter alia* in longer-term programme lending. This will mean that when it comes to establishing 'jointly shared guarantees' between OPEC and developed countries in phase two, an embryonic institutional mechanism involving 'shared guarantees' between OPEC and other developing countries will already have been in phase. The task of phase two could then be to accelerate evolution towards the final institutional form of phase three since what is involved would be the *addition* of a developed country guarantee element and only a *redefinition* of OPEC and other guarantees that will have already been operative.

Illustratively if programme lending were to proceed on the same terms as the World Bank's 'Third Window', viz. 4 per cent interest and 25-year maturity and market rates of borrowing are 8 per cent — approximately the rate on Deutsche-Mark denominated bonds, then it would take a 'once for all contribution' of $1 to generate $4 worth of lending provided the latter is supported by a system of limited, joint and several guarantees. If the capital of $4 can be raised in this way in the markets the problem is how the $1 for interest subsidy purposes is to be raised without burdening government budgets.

Three solutions suggest themselves. The first is to take advantage of the fact that we are today in the middle of an allocation of Special Drawing Rights to countries. The arrangement is that between 1979 and 1981 $12 billion SDR would be allocated at the rate of SDR $4 billion per year. We are today in the second tranche of this round of allocations. Each allocation is split up under the Fund Articles among developed and developing countries in proportion to their IMF quotas. But if a significant part of what now accrues to the developed countries this year and the next were to be *voluntarily* allocated to interest subsidy purposes (implementing in effect a 'link' mechanism for these purposes) then it would generate a substantial amount of lending on 'Third Window' terms. Nor need the decision await an amendment to IMF Articles because the national currency counterpart of SDRs can be used. Illustratively, if SDR $2 billion of the SDR allocation for each of the years 1980 and 1981 were to be set apart for interest subsidy purposes then annual programme lending on 'Third Window' terms of SDR $8 billion could easily be supported — or a total of SDR $16 billion for the remaining years of the current round of SDR allocations, provided a system of limited joint and several guarantees among *governments* to support borrowing on this scale can be set up as previously envisaged.

The second extra-budgetary solution to the interest subsidy problem that is spoken of is to dispose gradually of the gold that is available in the IMF. Some portion of it is already being sold, but there is the argument that some part of the balance can be sold off so as to generate an interest subsidy for quite substantial amounts of lending.

The third solution would be to treat the $2.4 billion with which it is intended to replenish the OPEC Special Fund this year as a 'once for all' interest subsidy contribution for programme lending on 'Third Window' terms. Assuming only that $2 billion would remain to be so used, a total lending this year of $8 billion becomes possible. All that would be required is for the OPEC countries to provide *in addition* a system of limited, joint and several guarantees to enable the Special Fund as presently constituted to borrow $8 billion in capital markets.[23] Indeed, its *further* transformation into a fully credit worthy development agency of an initial 'size' of $10 billion requires only an *additional* 'paid-in' capital of $2 billion as presently proposed by the governments of Algeria and Venezuela, $1 billion of which would comprise the present assets of the Special Fund in the form of loans outstanding to developing countries, the other $1 billion being paid in by OPEC countries on the commencement of operations. This provides not only for a 'safe' ratio of paid-in to total capital of 20 per cent being the ratio with which the World Bank commenced operations and considerably higher than the 7 per cent ratio underlying the current capital increase; it also enables developing countries to subscribe to the agency's paid-in capital as they redeem their debts to the Special Fund. The agency's initial callable capital of $8 billion would then constitute the system of joint and several guarantees against which up to $8 billion could be borrowed in the capital markets. The capital of the agency can of course be readily augmented without impairing its gearing ratio provided other groups of countries become willing to share in both paid-in and callable capital obligations.

Indeed, a combination of these three approaches alone for interest subsidy purposes – the use of available SDR allocations, of part of IMF gold and of expected replenishments to the OPEC Special Fund together with a system of supporting limited, joint and several guarantees to enable borrowing could generate in the years 1980–1 significantly large capital sums. This would serve both to initiate a process of 'massive transfers' to developing countries and with the addition of paid-in capital contributions to give it more permanent institutional form moving in the direction of the Brandt Commission's World Development Fund. Indeed, depending on the pace of evolution of events, the proposed transformation of the OPEC Special Fund into a Development Agency could well become the nucleus of the World Development

Fund itself. Whichever institutional route is taken towards implementing 'massive transfers' the key catalyst for action leading in this direction is the present compulsion on central banks to cooperate in dealing with reserve diversification pressures in the manner already described.

The consideration of a new institution for implementing massive transfer is obviously a question that has to be approached with caution and has indeed been so approached by the Brandt Commission. The relevant issue to raise is whether the tasks that are intended to be performed — e.g. longer-term programme lending — cannot be adequately discharged by tacking the functions on to either the World Bank or the IMF. The answer to this question embraces two categories of reasons. The first category groups together arguments which suggest that existing institutions cannot do the job of disbursing funds either fast enough or without prejudice to their traditional roles. The second category of arguments suggests that a new institution will offer certain 'innovative' possibilities in terms of operation which cannot easily be grafted on to existing institutions.

In regard to the first category of arguments, it is necessary to consider how far it applies to the principal existing institutions. Taking first the World Bank, the principal consideration that comes to mind is that its ethos is essentially one of project lending and that in the past, project disbursements have been slow whereas the exigencies of the global economic situation today calls for rapidly disbursing programme loans. There is also the question whether the Bank alone can very rapidly evolve the relevant performance criteria which relate to programme lending which of course are much more within the province of the IMF.

If one looks alternatively to the IMF for this essential reason, there is a very decisive argument to be countered which goes back to the previous history of these two institutions. Whatever might have been the view about the kind of institution that would have been desirable in 1945, there is today, so far as many developed countries are concerned, the feeling that an institution which deals with monetary stabilization ought not to convert itself into anything savouring of a long-term *development* institution; whatever the merits of the argument there is no doubt that the concern is real.

It was given expression to most recently by Mr De la Rosiere the Managing Director of the IMF in his speech to the Manila UNCTAD, where he argued that there is a limit to lending beyond the medium term which in his judgement the IMF ought not to cross. The argument is stated explicitly as follows:[24]

> In certain circumstances and in the case of those countries that are deeply embedded in underdevelopment, domestic policy adjustments would not be sufficient — even if they are supported by considerable *medium-term credits*. In such cases, *monetary mechanisms* must not be used alone as there is the risk of their breaking down or causing members to endure intolerable levels of deflation. It is the transfer of real resources that is at issue.

The implication quite clearly is that *longer-term* programme lending is outside IMF territory and within the category of development assistance. Indeed, the fear is that if the Fund is pushed too far into conventional development assistance territory — and there is a feeling that the Extended Fund Facility has gone far enough already — it might forfeit the confidence of developed countries who might be encouraged to establish their separate 'monetary' institution which would be unfortunate from the standpoint of international economic cooperation. Nevertheless, the crucial problem remains that development assistance of the conventional kind, namely through the medium of government budgets, is unlikely to materialize in the near future on the scale required for the reasons previously indicated. This is why an inevitable implication of massive transfer is the need to evolve some way of mobilizing resources in capital markets outside of government budgets.

In addition to this argument that the transformation of the IMF into a development institution is likely to undermine its role as a 'monetary mechanism' there is the consideration that the whole bias of the Fund tends towards looking at 'monetary' and stabilization questions much more than at the questions of planning and allocation of resources over a longer term which are the concern of the Bank.

It is true that these longer-term concerns have begun to preoccupy the Fund as it implements the Extended Facility, but in practice the 'planning' dimension has been sought to be met by liaising more closely with the Bank. What this leads on to is that ideally there ought to be elements of 'Fund' thinking as well as 'Bank' thinking in any institutional design that looks to evolving the kinds of conditions that are relevant for the disbursement of longer-term programme loans.

It is this challenge — the need to explore the analytically and operationally 'innovative' possibilities of conditionality which therefore constitutes the second category of arguments for any new institution. For the plain fact is that conditionality as practised *separately* in the Fund and in the Bank does not seem to be appropriate to the countries that receive monies; the Extended Fund Facility where close coordination between the Fund and the Bank is being attempted has found remarkably few customers. What is specially interesting in current discussions is the recognition of this constraint — at least as far as the IMF is concerned — by the banking community. What is argued is that because the banks unaided cannot do the job of recycling, conditions which inhibit countries from approaching the IMF sufficiently early ought to be relaxed. Thus Morgan Guaranty has urged that one such area of relaxation could be 'to increase the proportion of IMF resources available on reduced or minimal conditionality'.[25] In other words, what has been suggested here is that the fund resources under first credit tranche conditionality ought to be rather larger than is permitted by current practices. Many of these issues might with advantage be looked at by an institution that is intermediate yet somewhat distanced from both the Bank and the IMF but which can draw on the experience that these institutions have.

There is a second area in which an 'innovative' approach to conditionality can be evolved, namely that of isolation, in any particular balance of payments deficit of a developing country, the contribution of the so-called 'structural' element to that deficit from the 'policy' element. If the balance of payments deficit of a country is the result of running an 'excessive' government budget deficit and an over-rapid expansion of money supply, it ought to be possible to isolate the contribution to external imbalance of these 'policies'. But there is in the generality of cases another part of the balance of payments deficit which can in some notional sense be related to structural surpluses that other countries run — their formal counterpart so to speak. There would, in other words, be structural balance of payments deficits as the counterpart to some parts of OPEC and of other developed countries surplus. While the differences *in principle* between policy induced and structural balance of payments deficits will be readily acknowledged there is a genuine area of policy work to be done in separating out the different elements in any *particular* deficit. Once the distribution is made operationally the short answer policy-wise would be that the 'structural deficit' should be *unconditionally financed* because its persistence depends on actions being taken by surplus countries to eliminate their surpluses; correspondingly it is the 'policy induced' component of the deficit of a developing country that requires *adjustment* over an appropriately extended period of time and supporting financing of the 'adjustment programme'. There is no reason in principle why the analytical work required for determining the relevant degrees of conditionality should not be done within either established institution. But a new institution might respond to this challenge in a manner which has so far eluded established institutions — though it would require to work in the closest cooperation with the staffs of these institutions.

Perhaps most decisive of all in this second category of arguments relating to the 'innovative' role of a new institution is the issue of decision-making which goes to the heart of the matter. It would be fair to say that many developing countries deal with the established institutions in terms of an 'us' vs. 'them' set of attitudes. The institution is invariably perceived as being a foreign and alien body laying down terms to a recipient country which are viewed as flying in the face of domestic economic and social realities. Contributing heavily to this perception is the heavy weightage of developed countries in both voting within these institutions as well as in their staffing along with, of course, the pressures to over-rapid adjustment that result from the current range of available facilities. If one had an institution whose decision-making was based much more on consensus and a more equitably shared decision-making power between developed and developing countries that would *also* be providing programme lending on *substantially longer* terms, then it would be possible to argue that what is involved in conditionality is no more than a process of self-discipline by developing countries themselves. Different formulas could apply to different kinds of decision-making; while consensus could govern decisions relating to loans to particular developing countries, qualified majorities could prevail in matters concerning the raising of monies in the capital markets. Indeed, this kind of distinction is already to be found in the articles of the existing institutions. But the fundamental point remains that any institution that disposes of money has to lay down conditions, and that those conditions have both to be perceived as being desirable and accepted by those who are at the receiving end no less than by those who raise the money for its functioning. There is all the difference in the world between having an institution that is thought of as being equitable from the outset and coming reluctantly to terms with institutions as they are or as they gradually and tardily transform themselves. These considerations constitute to my mind the decisive argument for a new approach institutionally to the problem of conditionality which will serve as a catalyst for the transformation of existing structures.

Annexe A

Alternative guarantee arrangements

At least three types of guarantee arrangements are open to governments to establish among themselves for the purpose of underwriting any flotations of bonds raised in the capital markets, irrespective of whether they are to underpin any permanent new development agency.

The first and simplest type of guarantee would be a 'full

joint and several guarantee' of the bonds of the participating governments. Each government would, under such a guarantee, be liable for the *full* amount of the guaranteed obligations and a bondholder could make a claim against any single guarantor for the *full* amount due. The guarantor governments could, by arrangement, determine the proportion of their respective liabilities as among themselves, and any guarantor paying a bondholder more than its agreed share could recover from the other guarantors.

Secondly, and at the other extreme, would be a 'several guarantee' under which each government would guarantee only a specified proportion of each bond. This would present greater difficulty for bondholders since, unless special arrangements were made, it would be necessary in the event of a default to make a claim against *each* guarantor government.

A third and intermediate possibility would be an arrangement under which each member government, while giving only a several guarantee, would contribute, in an amount based on the proportion of the bonds guaranteed by it, to a fund in which the bondholders would share if there were a default. This approach is illustrated by the Austrian Government Guaranteed Loan (1923–43) arranged by the Financial Committee of the League of Nations. The net effect of such an arrangement would have many of the characteristics of, but would fall short of, a full joint and several guarantee. It is this third approach which may be described as a 'limited joint and several guarantee'.

This type of guarantee would be somewhat similar to the arrangement by which the member governments of any Development Agency 'guarantee' that Agency's obligations on the basis of its callable capital. Strictly speaking, bonds issued by the Agency are not guaranteed by the Agency's member governments. However, in case of a default on its bonds, or to prevent a default, the Agency can call for payment of the callable as distinct from paid-in capital of its member governments and use the amounts received to make the required payments on its bonds. Each government's obligation to make payments on such calls is not dependent on payment being made by other member governments and, since successive calls may be made until sufficient funds are available to pay the obligations of the Agency, the system is very like a joint and several guarantee. But since each government is liable only to the extent of its uncalled capital, such a system is not equivalent to a full joint and several guarantee, as no *single* government can be liable for the total amount being guaranteed by all participating governments together.

It follows from this account of possible guarantee mechanisms that any desired system of guarantees can be established among participating governments prior to the formal setting up of the Agency. Indeed, in the case of the proposed Development Agency, it is open to interested OPEC governments to establish a system of 'limited, joint and several guarantees' along the lines of the Austrian Loan Guarantee procedure referred to above. This would enable them to raise monies pending the formal establishment of a Development Agency in a manner which would obviate the need in the transitional year for the formal putting in of capital subscriptions other than the amounts required for the interest subsidy element. Such a system could also be set up pending the subsequent joining in with the Agency of governments who may not initially participate. This would, in principle, enable interested governments to put together *only* the cash amounts required for the interest subsidy element leaving the OPEC Special Fund as presently constituted not only to discharge the task of disbursing funds, but also enabling the Special Fund itself to float bonds in the capital market on the strength solely of the guarantees being provided by interested governments.

Notes

1 UNCTAD: United Nations Conference on Trade and Development.
2 UNCTAD V Resolution 129 (V), *The Transfer of Real Resources to Developing Countries* (3 June 1979). Part IV, Massive Transfer of Resources.
3 UNCTAD V, *Arusha Programme for Collective Self-Reliance and Framework for Negotiations*, Manila, May 1979, p. 50.
4 Commission of the European Communities, *Annual Economic Review 1978-79*, Brussels, 19 October 1978, p. 8.2. Emphasis added.

5 Commission of the European Communities, *Europe and the Third World – A Study on Interdependence*, Brussels, February 1979, pp. 53 and 54.
6 Ibid.
7 Dr Seipp, Speech on the occasion of a Press Conference convened in connection with the presentation of the financial statement of West Deutsche Landesbank International S.A., Luxembourg, 10 January 1980.
8 Rimmer de Vries, 'The International Monetary Outlook for 1980 – No time for Complacency', *World Financial Markets* (Morgan Guaranty), December 1979. De Vries' scenarios imply cumulative OPEC surpluses for the period 1979 to 1983 in the range of $380 billion to $460 billion.
9 Reuters, telegram dated 25 January 1980. Emphasis added.
10 Seipp, op. cit.
11 Rimmer de Vries, op. cit., p. 7.
12 *The Amex Bank Review*, 22, vol. 5, no. 9, September 1978.
13 *The Financial Times*, 19 March 1979.
14 Rimmer de Vries, op. cit.
15 *The Times*, 'Oil Money: Unbalance the Banking System', London, 7 January 1980.
16 *The Reserve Assets Study Group of the Group of Thirty: Reserve Assets and a Substitution Account: Towards a Less Unstable International Monetary System*, February 1980, p. 19.
17 See ibid., p. 18. 'An alternative or complementary approach to the balance of payments channel is the foreign currency substitution channel. Problems posed by the relative lack of development of surplus countries' capital markets might also, to some extent, be avoided by this approach which allows for diversification outside the markets. For example, the strong currency countries could issue obligations in their own currencies in exchange for dollar claims on the United States. The advantages would be that they could thereby arguably sterilize the domestic monetary effects of foreign currency inflows before they actually occurred; that such techniques would be independent of the state of the countries' domestic financial markets; and that if the claims were in the form of long-term placements with central banks they could be less volatile than short-term capital inflows. This approach might be considered analogous to a swap, with one leg of it in longer-term assets. However, strong currency countries would under this proposal have to accept further accumulations of dollar reserves and presumably the resultant exchange risk, unless bilateral arrangements are agreed between participating countries to share

the exchange risk or the strong currency countries deposited newly-acquired dollar reserves in the Substitution Account'.

18 Independent Commission on International Development Issues, *North-South: A Programme for Survival*, London, 1980, p. 279.
19 See Annexe A.
20 World Bank, *World Development Report 1979*, p. 32.
21 W. Randolph Burgess, testimony before US House of Representatives Banking and Currency Committee, 21 March. Emphasis added.
22 See above, p. 49.
23 See Annexe A.
24 J. de la Rosiere, *Address before UNCTAD V*, Manila, May 1979. Emphasis added.
25 Morgan Guaranty Trust, 'In quest of International Monetary Stability', *World Financial Markets*, October 1979, p. 12.

4 OPEC SURPLUS FUND

Robert Mabro*

1 Introduction

The long debate on OPEC surplus funds began in earnest in early 1977. Economists and bankers developed an interest in this issue well before the dramatic oil price rises of October 1973–January 1974. A significant rise in the price of oil, the inevitable consequence of an 'impending energy crisis', was widely forecast several months before it occurred. Those who predicted the oil price revolution soon realized that OPEC increased foreign exchange revenues will exceed foreign exchange expenditures. The balance of payments of several OPEC member countries will be in surplus. The same experts argue that oil prices will continue to rise over a long period. They also felt that the absorptive capacity, loosely defined as the ability to spend, will remain constrained for many years. Hence, the alarming conclusions: the surplus is chronic in nature, the annual surplus will increase from year to year, the accumulated surpluses will threaten the stability of the international banking system, the international monetary order and the world economy.

We heard it all in seminars as early as May 1973, we read it all in newspaper articles and in more serious publications throughout 1974 and 1975. The issue has been continually debated since then with more or less interest and conviction, the interest reviving after every significant rise in the price of oil and receding during periods of stagnation.

Naturally every participant in the debate has been looking at the issue from his own narrow point of view. Bankers

* Mr. R. Mabro is a fellow of St. Anthony's College, Oxford University, England.

expressed worries about their ability to absorb large and increasing deposits. They warned about the dangers of growing liabilities carried on the foundation of a small capital base. As growing deposits induced an expansion in lending they wondered whether they will find sufficient credit-worthy borrowers or whether they will have to lower continually their sights and lend increasing amounts to less credit-worthy customers.

Western economists were concerned about the impact of chronic and significant imbalances in world payments. True, recycling always takes place *ex post*. But the serious economic problems — deflation, beggar-my-neighbour policies, etc. — arise from *ex ante* behaviour. Countries faced with the prospects of a deficit may try to reduce its size and sacrifice economic growth in the process. Imbalances resulting from the OPEC surplus funds can plunge the world economy into severe and prolonged recession.

Economists concerned with the welfare of developing countries exhorted OPEC countries to divert their surplus funds to the Third World. The late Fred Hirsh, who has innumerable followers, was the first to do so in an open letter to King Feisal published in the British Press in early 1974.

Less serious, often less innocent, writers rang the alarm bell. They argued that the surplus funds would constitute a 'money weapon'. The Arabs would use this weapon by suddenly shifting their deposits from one currency to another, bringing chaos to the foreign exchange markets. The truth, however, is the other way round. The depositor of large sums has no weapon to wield because he has handed over his weapon for safe-keeping to his potential victim.

The least vocal participants in the debate are the OPEC countries themselves. Their views about surplus funds, though expressed both in speeches and in writing, do not receive the same publicity; and many a serious student of the subject can plead ignorance.

I do not propose in this chapter to survey the position of bankers, Western politicians, economists and aid lobbyists. Several papers in this project tackle the important issues raised by surplus funds for the banking system, world economic growth and the welfare of poor countries.

The purposes, rather, are (a) to identify and analyse the position of oil-producing countries as regard surplus funds, (b) to discuss certain aspects of the issue which have not been sufficiently emphasized or clarified in the current debate, (c) to study the factors which may determine the future course of events, mainly the size of future surpluses and the investment strategies likely to be pursued by the oil-producing countries.

2   Oil-producing countries and surplus funds

Petroleum is a non-reproducible mineral resource. The size of the ultimate recoverable stock available to an oil-producing country is never known with great precision. Some countries, for example Kuwait, have been fairly well surveyed and explored, and the assessment of availabilities is accordingly less uncertain than in other countries. Much exploration and development remains to be done in Iraq and Saudi Arabia, and it is almost certain that ultimate availabilities are significantly greater than current assessments suggest.

Nevertheless, all oil-producing countries are acutely aware that (a) oil is a wasting asset, (b) the life of their reserves, however long, remains shorter than the many decades required for economic development. The first perception would be irrelevant if the second perception were incorrect or unduly pessimistic. Much hinges therefore on the assessment of the time required to establish an alternative economic base to oil, an economic structure capable of generating and sustaining high levels of income and a reasonable rate of economic growth. There is no doubt in my mind that the development horizon, as defined in the preceding sentence, lies well ahead of us. The Gulf countries, with their small populations and their barren lands, are unlikely to achieve the goals of their long-term development in less than 50, if not 70 or 80 years.

The perception that oil is an exhaustible resource is therefore relevant to the understanding of attitudes and policies in petroleum-exporting countries. Governments relate, in their thinking at least, oil policies (production, pricing, exploration and development of oilfields) and development strategies involving fundamental structural changes over the long term.

Oil is seen as a commodity in the markets where it is traded. It is also seen as a commodity by the buyers who ultimately consume it in a wide variety of uses. Oil, however, is seen as an asset by the owner of the resource. Similarly, for all assets, the value of the stock of oil held in the form of natural reserves can appreciate or depreciate over time. If the producer treats oil exclusively as an asset then his production decision is akin to a portfolio management decision. As Hotelling taught us, there is an optimum rate of production which equates the rate of change of the oil price with the rate of interest. On the equilibrium path, the present value of the stock of assets remains constant if all the revenues from production are invested for a return equal to the rate of interest. The Hotelling rule has little operational value in a world beset with uncertainties of all kinds. One of its merits, however, is to spell out the implications of treating oil as an asset. Strict adherence to the logic of the producer's position (oil is an asset and we badly need to maintain the aggregate present value of all our assets given our concern for economic development) would require (a) the pursuit in the best possible manner of a portfolio-orientated production policy, and (b) the reinvestment of all the proceeds from petroleum exports.

The latter is not possible for the simple reason that oil-producing countries have no significant source of income outside the petroleum sector. They have no choice but to live off their capital. Their objective therefore is not the extreme injunction 'reinvest it all', but the more moderate 'reinvest as much as you can'.

A surplus in the balance of payments on current account arises when revenues exceed the import requirements of consumption, intermediate demand and domestic investment. The surplus, by definition, is for reinvestment. The balance of payments surplus of an oil-producer is not perceived in the same way as the surplus of an industrialized country. In one case, the surplus arises from the sale of a domestic asset and is used to purchase foreign assets held abroad. In the latter case the surplus arises from imbalances in external transactions involving commodities rather than assets, and surpluses accumulated in reserves are not primarily regarded as permanent assets in the national portfolio but as transaction balances carried over from good to bad years. Of course, an interest is earned on transaction balances; this interest, however, is the lowest form of return.

The oil-producing country with a financial surplus is in fact trading oil in the ground for paper claims on foreign assets (either monetary or real). The rate of appreciation of oil in the ground is unknown. Oil-producing countries believe that this rate is higher than the return on their foreign assets. One cause of pessimism is the need to discount assets held abroad because of the risks of confiscation. The freezing of Iranian assets in the US confirmed the Gulf countries' worst fears. The incident showed that (a) freezing is a very easy decision to take, (b) once taken, the decision has very entangled repercussions in the world banking system, (c) the US has little control over the effects of freezing which makes 'unfreezing' a very complex task, (d) bankers whom you trust rather than politicians whom you may distrust induce the freezing decision.

Portfolio options available to oil-producing countries are also limited, and so is the number of financial places in the world capable of dealing with large transactions. Purchase of real assets has increased over the years, but the share of real assets in the foreign portfolio of oil-producing countries remains small. For political reasons, oil-producing countries prefer to keep a low profile and tend to avoid massive purchases of equity and real estate which could induce restrictive legislation in the host countries.

All in all, holding money abroad is not terribly attractive. It is a residual option, the only one left after investment at home has been pushed to the limits of absorptive capacity. But the residual option also sets the opportunity cost. If the returns on assets held abroad are very low or negative, it becomes difficult to persuade the oil-producing countries that the rate of appreciation of oil in the ground is even lower. Even if they allowed for many uncertainties they would still feel that their credibility is being stretched a bit too far.

It would seem, therefore, that the option is to avoid surpluses. Governments of oil-producing countries if asked about their preferences would probably say that they want to generate sufficient current revenues from petroleum exports to finance the import contents of a preferred volume of investment in the national economy and of the associated consumption and intermediate expenditures. But let us examine in detail the meaning of such desires. Countries with small volumes of production, small petroleum reserves and large populations need to generate large oil revenues. They tend to produce at full capacity and seek the highest possible prices. They do not worry very much about the substitution effects of high prices, and their impact on future oil income. They believe that substitution away from oil is a slow process, and they know that the life of their reserves is relatively short. However, the small oil countries are, by definition, price-takers. They cannot set the international price of oil precisely because they are small producers. They are vocal within OPEC and the world outside considers them as militant. To equate militancy and power would be a mistake. The situation as described so far can be summed up in a few words. The small oil-producers need the revenues and prefer to maximize them through prices rather than quantities. But they are price-takers by virtue of their size. In recent years they benefited from the price effects of market power vested in other OPEC producers. Despite the high oil revenues thus obtained the small oil producer (small in this paragraph is to be understood both in terms of market share and relative to population) usually suffers from balance of payments deficits. Typical illustrations are Algeria, Indonesia, Ecuador and on occasions Nigeria and Venezuela.

Oil-producing countries with small populations divide into two groups. Some are small oil-producers in terms of their market share (e.g. Qatar) but large in per capita terms. Others are large producers in terms of market share (e.g. Saudi Arabia) and still large in per capita terms. The small producer with a small population tends to behave in the market-place like a small producer with a large population.

The small producer irrespective of other circumstances is a price-taker. He also tends to appear as a price-militant in

OPEC deliberations. There are, however, other differences in behaviour between small producers depending on their population size. The small producer with a smaller population is inherently a conservationist. He does not seek production at full capacity. On the contrary, the objective is a low rate of depletion and a lengthening of the expected life of the reserve. The conservationist faces, however, the uncertain business prospects of the long term. High oil prices through an acceleration of the substitution process may put oil out of business well before the end of the extended depletion period of his reserves.

The upshot of this discussion is simple: oil-producing countries enjoying a surplus have little room for manœuvre in matters of balance of payments equilibrium. Those afflicted with a deficit can perhaps do something about it through a reduction in imports. At first there is no incentive to do so. Oil enhances credit-worthiness and makes the raising of substantial foreign loans a relatively easy affair. Taking advantage of the opportunity makes a lot of sense. But indebtedness accumulates over the years and chronic deficits, sooner or later, begin to be perceived as a serious problem. Even then, the remedy — import cuts — is not easy to administer. It can have traumatic socio-political effects. Countries with a surplus are in a tighter fix. They may or may not want their surpluses. In either case there is little they can do about it. To import more than they do would choke their economic machines. To export less oil is possible up to a point. Kuwait has already gone as far as it can. Qatar has still marginal room for manœuvre, so small, however, as to be negligible. Abu Dhabi could easily impose lower limits on offtake. Kuwait did not succeed in eliminating the surplus. Abu Dhabi would still have a sizeable surplus should it decide to reduce output to the practical minimum. In any case, as mentioned earlier, Saudi Arabia will always find it difficult to implement a balance of payments policy because the role of residual supplier is played in priority. If the real world were that of economic theorists, oil-producing countries would attempt first to get their depletion policy right. The revenues generated through the implementation of an optimum depletion policy would then be allocated between present and future consumption (i.e. investment) according to well-known propositions elaborated by Irving Fisher and Hirshfleir. The amount allocated to investment would then be divided between domestic capital accumulation and foreign placements in a way that would equate marginal returns in alternative outlets. Enlightened theorists would probably allow a discount for 'security' on returns on foreign placements. Theory is useful in that it provides a norm, a sort of null hypothesis, which helps in identifying the causes and magnitudes of deviations.

Because the future is fairly opaque, it is virtually impossible to pursue an optimum production policy. Oil-exporting countries are also hindered by other considerations: commercial (oligopolists are always concerned with their market shares), technical (a minimum level of production must be maintained to ensure the long-term productivity of oilfields and to obtain the amounts of associated gas required by the domestic economy), political (pressures from powerful oil-consuming nations). What remains true, however, is that the production policy (meaning in this context both output and prices) is a prime determinant. Expenditures respond to revenues up to the limits vaguely defined by the economy's absorptive capacity. If the level of expenditures is too high, physical bottlenecks and other manifestations of supply inelasticities cause inflation and material waste. Governments respond after two or three years by drastic curtailment of public expenditures. If the reaction is then judged to be excessive they engage in further adjustments until a correct feel of the true limits of absorptive capacity is gained.

The logical (not, of course, the chronological) sequence, therefore, is: production which yields revenues, expenditures that are partly autonomous and largely induced, and a surplus emerging in the end as a mere residual. There is no explicit attempt to equate or compare returns on the investment at home and placements abroad whether at the margin or inside it. If the limits of absorptive capacity are defined in terms of a maximum tolerable inflation rate or in terms of a maximum rate of workers' immigration, the cut-off point for domestic investment would not necessarily involve a rate of return comparable to that on foreign placements. The former might turn out to be higher or lower than the latter. It would even be negative in certain heavy-industry ventures and in some infrastructural projects.

Like any economic agent, governments of oil-producing countries attempt to do their best in an imperfect world. They would dearly like to follow an optimum production policy. As they lack room for manœuvre on output they tend to concentrate on prices. Their achievements on that score are impressive, which does not mean that they approach the optimum course.

They would dearly like to follow an optimum expenditure policy. But they are subjected on that front to enormous pressures both from within their economy and from outside. They would dearly like to invest sensibly their surplus funds. Let us now examine in detail their objectives and policies in this field, the opportunities available to them and the constraints.

The objectives are those of any investor: high and secure returns. There is a trade-off between gains and security. Further, the issue of security arises at two levels. There is, *first*, a general problem of political insecurity inherent in the fact that a foreign placement is held abroad. This problem cannot be eliminated entirely except through repatriation which, by definition, is impossible. The only options are either to hedge by diversifying your outlets or to seek a political or institutional insurance in the form of international guarantees. The oil-producing countries have opted for diversification. In 1973 their portfolio was heavily concentrated in the US. Today the holdings are spread in a few major centres: New York, London, Zurich, Frankfurt and to a much lesser extent Paris, Tokyo and Singapore. The complex international web of banking subsidiaries and joint banking ventures makes it impossible to define clearly the boundaries of national jurisidiction in the world financial system. The investor may well believe that his monies are deposited in London and then find that they fall within the US orbit. As mentioned earlier, there are inherent limits to diversification simply because the international financial system is fairly concentrated. Oil-producing countries have

never seriously explored the second option, that of international guarantees. One reason is that no attractive scheme
was ever proposed for their consideration. Several ideas
have been advanced by individuals — intellectually-inclined
bankers, academics, financial journalists. None had the backing of those governments and official agencies which are
supposed to provide the guarantees. Another reason is that
the counterpart of international guarantees in many a scheme
is some loss of investor's autonomy. The oil-producing countries find this feature unpalatable.

The *second* aspect of security is purely commercial.
A deposit in a large bank is in some sense more secure than
a placement in a small financial institution. An industrialized
country is more credit-worthy than a developing nation.
Further, some industrialized countries, notably the US and
the UK, happen to supply large quantities of marketable
government paper (which is, perhaps, why the financial
markets are so developed in these two countries). Other
industrialized countries have much less, and developing
nations virtually nothing, to offer in this area. A risk-averse
investor will prefer bonds to equities, and within equities
will always concentrate on blue-chip shares.

It is not surprising that oil-producing countries placed
initially most of their funds in liquid deposits with a few
major international (read US with a sprinkling of UK) banks
or in US/UK government securities. Diversification of the
portfolio then proceeded cautiously and slowly, but the
movement has become significant over the years. SAMA,
the Saudi Central Bank, deals now with some eighty banks.
The Kuwaitis, thanks to their very long experience of international finance, have managed to diversify their portfolio,
both geographically and by type of assets, in a very significant way. When asked about their investment policy the
Kuwaitis now invariably reply: we are doing very nicely,
thank you. They see no merit in any further discussion of
the issue.

Oil-producing countries distinguish sharply between aid to
developing countries and financial placements. The latter aim
at commercial returns with a heavy trade-off for security.
The former is an instrument of foreign policy. Oil-producing

countries do not believe that political risks associated with commercial placements are smaller in developing than in industrialized countries. They also think that save for a few projects in a few countries the commercial opportunities are very limited in the Third World. Risk-aversion is strong. If a choice is offered between an equity holding in Volvo and an equity participation in a car-assembly plant in Brazil, one may choose Brazil for higher returns and Volvo for greater security. Such is the trade-off that the oil-producing country will invariably settle for the Volvo holding.

Aid belongs to a different sphere. Several attempts have been made to persuade Gulf countries of the existence of a link between profitable investments of surpluses and cooperation with the Third World. The case is familiar to this audience. The schemes proposed are varied and imaginative. Some emphasize bilateral complementarities: OPEC finance and Third World natural resources, OPEC markets and Third World industries, OPEC industrialization and Third World labour and skills. Others emphasize trilateral complement-arities: OPEC finance, Western/Japanese technology, Third World resources. Unfortunately, one cannot report much progress on this front. One is also at a loss explaining this lack of success except by a fairly rigid separation of spheres (aid belonging to the ethico-political and placements to the financial/commercial sphere). This explanation deserves more questions than it purports answers.

It is possible, of course, that the process of learning which led to greater diversification of the portfolio held in Western institutions will slowly extend to a wider diversification involving the Third World. The separation of two activities need not remain rigidly fixed for ever. New ideas eventually sink in. A timid experiment at crossing the border, if success-ful, would lead to other experiments and the border will cease to be an insuperable barrier once it has been crossed repeatedly. Progress in this area will depend more on con-crete ventures than on philosophical preaching. The Third World government which succeeds in persuading Saudi Arabia or Kuwait to join in a bilateral or trilateral venture and makes a success of it will do more for the cause than volumes of academic discussion. The difficulty met by those who promote the various concepts of cooperation is that they arouse suspicion. If the promoters are citizens of the Third World, they immediately appear as interested parties. If the promoters are Western, they will be suspected of hypocrisy. For the West has done its utmost to damage the prospects of cooperation between oil-producers and the Third World by consistently suggesting since 1973 that the rich man's burden should now become the oil-producers' responsibility. This attitude has profoundly inhibiting effects.

3   Some facts about surplus funds

There are, first, problems of definition. A broad concept equates surplus funds with the net annual excess of total foreign exchange revenues and total foreign exchange current expenditures (excluding official unrequited transfers). This aggregate is larger than the balance of payments surplus on current account. A more restrictive definition, useful for the study of recycling problems, equates surplus funds with the amounts invested abroad by the oil-producing countries. Soft loans to developing countries are part of the current account surplus, but not a component of surplus funds.

It must be emphasized that the common practice which treats all OPEC countries as a single entity is absurd. To talk about OPEC surpluses is absurd. Some OPEC countries suffer from chronic deficits. Some enjoy surpluses for a very short period of time (e.g. only in 1974 and in 1979/80; immediately after a significant oil price rise) and then move into deficit. A few have consistently enjoyed surpluses since the beginning of the 1970s, and Kuwait may have been in surplus year in, year out since the mid-1950s. Saudi Arabia which usually has the largest annual surplus (in dollar terms) and which possesses the largest stock of accumulated funds barely managed to balance its external accounts in 1978.

Further, the surplus of one OPEC country is not offset by the deficit of another. It is as misleading to speak of OPEC surpluses as it is of OECD aggregate balance. What is important in the latter case is that the UK is in surplus and that France, the US and Germany are in deficit. Similarly what matters in the OPEC case is the position of individual countries.

There are enormous problems with statistics. Balance of payments data are difficult to reconcile with banking and investment figures. To make things worse, world trade never balances in the statistical books.

The best available data present the following picture;

Table 4.1   Annual surpluses/deficits of oil-producing countries

Year	Surpluses $US billion	Deficits $US billion	Net external borrowings and residuals
1974	67	—	−12
1975	30	−1	7
1976	37	2	4
1977	33	−6	11
1978	13	−14	20
1979	74	—	5

Column 1 includes surpluses of high absorbers (Algeria, Indonesia, etc.) which accrued to them only in 1974 and in 1979. These amount to $20 billion. Some of the surpluses in column 1 should also be offset against occasional deficits incurred by middle-absorbers (Iran, etc.). I would tentatively estimate this latter item at $5 billion. The accumulated surpluses of 'true' OPEC surplus countries (1974–9 inclusive) could then be estimated at $254 billion − $25 billion = $229 billion. The Bank of England aggregates surpluses and deficits and adds net external borrowings to arrive at the concept of 'cash surplus available for investment'. I am more concerned with 'own' surplus funds of individual countries than with gross cash surpluses. Cash available for investment adds up to $266 billion according to the Bank's calculations. Not surprisingly, however, the Bank can only identify $236 billion in the allocation of placements.

The distribution of placements is shown in Table 4.2. If aid and placements are distinguished and if contributions to the IMF and the IBRD are treated in this context as placements, true surplus funds accumulation (i.e. assets owned by oil-producing countries and available to them for future use) was $198 billion by the end of 1979. From the

Table 4.2   Distribution of placements

	$ billion	%
Bank deposits	115	49
of which Euro-currency	(89)	(38)
Short-term Govt. Securities	7	3
Long-term Govt. Securities	10	4
Other portfolio investment	58	25
of which real assets (est.)	(25)	(10)
IMF facilities and IBRD bonds	8	3
Loans to developing countries	38	16
Total	236	100%

point of view of the Third World, both direct assistance and multilateral contributions constitute aid. In that sense the Third World has received directly 19.5 per cent of the OPEC surpluses.

Table 4.2 shows a distribution between real and financial assets. Leaving out loans to developing countries, the 'surplus fund' portfolio of $198 billion (end of 1979) includes only $25 billion of real assets, i.e. less than 13 per cent. In 1975 the percentage share of real assets may not have exceeded 2 or 3 per cent. There is improvement, and still a long way to go.

The main 'surplus' countries are: Saudi Arabia, Kuwait, Iraq, the UAE, Libya and Qatar. Because of the Gulf war, Iraq surpluses will vanish and may not re-emerge for many years. Qatar's surpluses are very small. The only significant surpluses: first, the expansion in the absorptive capacity UAE and Libya. To all intents and purposes, the OPEC surpluses are the surpluses of four countries only. Within this small set, Saudi Arabia is by far the most considerable element.

4   Future developments

Three major factors influence in the long-term the size of surpluses: First, the expansion in the absorptive capacity of the oil-producing country; secondly, changes in the relative rate of oil price increases; thirdly, changes in the volume of world demand for OPEC oil.

The first force operates unabated over the long-run in any economy able to pursue peacefully its development objectives. Wars and revolutions upset the process. The Iranian revolution has reduced significantly, perhaps only temporarily, the absorptive capacity of the Iranian economy. The Gulf war, on the other hand, may well be followed by a period of reconstruction calling for significant increases in imports. In the short term, either because of exogenous shocks, or because of the 'trial-and-error' processes described earlier on, the propensity to import seems to behave in a very erratic manner. It will suffice to glance at Table 4.3 for a vivid illustration.

Table 4.3   Imports of oil exports. Percentage change on preceeding years

	1974	1975	1976	1977	1978	1979
Import volume	+40	+43	+23	+10	+4	−12
Import prices	+26	+7	+1	+10	+12	+15

Source: Bank of England.

In the long run, however, the expansion in the capacity to absorb imports will tend to dominate. If this factor alone was in operation the surpluses would vanish in a matter of years. History provides us with a precedent. The 1974–8 episode indicates that one oil price explosion leads to surpluses emerging and vanishing within five years. The second factor, the relative rate of oil price increases, is of considerable importance. Surpluses emerge whenever the oil price rises suddenly and significantly. These sudden rises are usually associated with a political accident. If the political accident adversely affects the capacity to import of one OPEC country, the combination of price increases and reduced import capacity produces a large surplus. Let us examine history once again. The Iranian revolution resulted in the significant price rises of 1979. The Gulf war induced much smaller price rises in late 1980. Iran produces much less oil since the revolution but it also imports much less stuff. Iraq and Iran are producing far less oil since the war, and though their import trade is hindered by the hostilities they are facing nevertheless the prospect of large deficits. Meanwhile, Saudi Arabia and other 'low-absorbers' Gulf countries increase their oil production to make good the Iranian/Iraqi shortfall. An Iranian deficit does not offset a portion of the Saudi surplus. An Iraqi deficit might, but the deficit is financed from past accumulation. The net effect of all these events is a considerable shift in favour of the hardcore surplus countries.

The third factor is world demand for OPEC oil. The long-term trend will depend on the relative strength of three opposing forces: conservation in use, economic growth and substitution. My own belief is that world demand for OPEC oil will decline very slowly over the next 20 years. Note, however, that cyclical and seasonal movements around the trend line can be extremely significant. This is a complicating factor in the short run resulting in revenue fluctuations and variability in the volume of annual surpluses.

To sum up. Two long-run tendencies — expanding absorptive capacity and an expected slow decline in the world demand for oil — suggest that time may erode the (current) surplus position of oil-producing countries. But the system is subjected to shocks: bursts of oil price increases and political accidents leading to shifts in the distribution of oil exports between high and low absorbers. Oil price explosions lead almost immediately to the emergence of significant surpluses, but in subsequent years import inflation together with other factors alters the balance. Distributional shifts can operate either way. In 1979–80 they favoured surplus countries. In 1981–2, when Iraq and Iran will be trying to export large quantities of oil at the expense of Saudi Arabia and other Gulf producers the shift may work against the surplus countries.

I would hate venturing a forecast. Surpluses in 1980 may well have totalled $90 billion. This may well turn out to be a peak year. The 1981 surplus is likely to be much smaller, $50–60 billion perhaps and 1982 may well resemble 1978 with a meagre surplus of $10–15 billion. Provided no political accident intervenes in the meantime pushing prices through some ceiling. The picture will change in the mid-1980s if the world economy recovers. Surpluses of $60–80 billion are conceivable then. A major price change anytime in this period could produce an abnormal surplus in an odd year of $100–200 billion. But I see no predictable trend, erratic ups and downs rather than regular behaviour.

5 Conclusions

The OPEC surpluses elicit more excitement than the issue deserves. The annual surpluses are not very large and in certain years they were indeed insignificantly small. The world financial system can absorb them with relative ease and recycle them *tant bien que mal*. To focus on the surpluses may distract attention from more serious problems, those facing weak economies struggling to finance their import bills.

There is no panacea to the ills of those countries. If OPEC countries stepped up their import programmes and corrected in this way the imbalance of their external accounts, the world economy might grow at a higher rate. Some industrialized, and perhaps a few Third World, countries would find it easier to balance their external books. It does not follow that all deficit countries would see their deficits vanish. The OPEC surplus could become somebody else's surplus rather than offset the deficit of weak economies.

Weak economies must be helped in the long and difficult period of adjustment to the oil price shock. This help is the responsibility of the entire international community: OECD, OPEC and the affected countries themselves. The OECD countries (there are exceptions of course) are not in a mood to help and every year that passes takes us downhill on the issue of international cooperation. The OPEC countries are extremely wary of open-ended commitments. All the good hearted and the less innocent Westerners who appeal to OPEC for more aid to the Third World in fact harm the prospects of aid. Hamish McRae, who is certainly well intentioned, wrote in *The Guardian* on 10 February 1981:

'. . . as the West's ability and willingness to provide aid is reduced it is vital that other sources (*read* OPEC) of development aid should be boosted' (p. 22). OPEC does not believe that the West's ability is impaired. It must be a matter of willingness. But if the West is unwilling, any increase in OPEC aid will tend to be matched by a further decrease in Western aid. Is OPEC asked to increase the resources available to the Third World or to release resources for the West?

Paradoxically, the surpluses are the surplus countries' problem. They reflect structural disequilibria within their economies. The surpluses reinforce the oil producers' dependence on certain Western powers and this increased external dependence is a further destabilizing force internally. Further, surplus cash, wealth in a liquid form, distorts perceptions. Some OPEC countries appear, and come themselves to believe, to be much richer than they are. This is the biggest curse of them all.

5   GOLD, SDRs AND DEVELOPING COUNTRIES

David A. Brodsky and Gary P. Sampson*

Abstract

International agreement was reached in the early 1970s that future creation of international reserves would be largely via SDR allocations, to be distributed to individual countries in proportion to their quotas in the IMF. In this manner, the international monetary system would play a 'neutral' role in the creation and distribution of international reserves. It has become increasingly apparent in recent years, however, that the international monetary system has been far from neutral in its distribution of international liquidity. The *de facto* revaluation of reserve asset gold has led to a massive creation of international reserves   nearly $500 billion by the end of 1979 — which has served to benefit almost exclusively the major gold-holding countries, all among the wealthiest of the industrialized nations.

Unlike the major gold-holding countries, which throughout the Bretton Woods era converted two-thirds of their foreign exchange holdings into gold, developing countries largely accepted the US pledge that the dollar was 'as good as gold'. As a result, the quantitative analysis presented in this chapter shows that developing countries have foregone reserve holdings in excess of $100 billion. To redress partially the inequitable distribution of international reserves which has arisen from the *de facto* revaluation of reserve asset gold — and at the same time to promote a significant transfer of resources to developing countries — this chapter proposes

* The authors are members of the Special Programme for Least Developed Countries and Manufactures Division, respectively, of the UNCTAD Secretariat. The views expressed in this chapter are their own and not necessarily those of UNCTAD.

the establishment of a 'Gold Account for Development' based on official gold holdings.

Introduction

The decade of the 1970s has seen many fundamental changes in the international monetary system. For the most part, however, such changes have occurred not in accordance with a thorough and comprehensive plan designed to meet the needs of all countries, but on an *ad hoc* basis, or without full international agreement. To a large extent the significant implications of such 'reforms', for both individual countries and the world economy as a whole, have yet to be fully appreciated.

In particular, recent events have shown that the international monetary system is rapidly moving in the direction of a *de facto* revaluation of reserve asset gold at a market-related price. Thus, while until December 1974 virtually all countries valued their gold reserves at an institutionally determined price,[1] during that month agreement was reached allowing individual countries to value their reserve asset gold at a price of their own determination. In the intervening years, nearly fifty countries, as well as the European Monetary Cooperation Fund (EMCF), have abandoned the former official price of gold in favour of a market-related valuation. Moreover, irrespective of the bookkeeping value placed on national holdings of reserve asset gold, there has been increasing evidence that the *effective* value of gold reserves is directly related to the market price.[2]

This development has no doubt come as a surprise to many, since a number of events in the late 1960s and early 1970s — including the establishment of the SDR as a new international reserve asset — had been widely interpreted as significantly reducing the prominent role which gold has long occupied in the international monetary system. Proposals to increase the level of world reserves by raising the official price of gold had been decisively rejected, largely on the grounds that the distribution among individual countries of the world's stock of reserve asset gold, and hence the gains to be realized through its revaluation, was highly uneven. This objection was, and remains today, a well-founded one, for it is difficult to discern anything optimal about the world distribution of reserve asset gold. On the contrary, a strong case can be made that the distribution of *gold* reserves has arisen largely as a matter of historical accident or, in several cases, as the result of efforts to undermine the 'dollar exchange standard' in the 1960s.

Nevertheless, as a result of the *de facto* revaluation of reserve asset gold, in recent years individual countries have received new international reserves, not in accordance with their needs or with any other rational criterion, but solely in proportion to their existing holdings of gold. The major beneficiaries of this unanticipated change in the international monetary system have been the principal gold-holding countries, all among the wealthiest of the industrialized nations, which by the end of the 1970s had accrued combined profits of nearly $340 billion. In the years to come these profits will be available for effecting a significant transfer of real resources in favour of these countries.

This chapter will show that the massive profits accumulated by the gold-holding countries — and hence the ensuing resource transfers — have occurred primarily at the expense of developing countries, which historically have held only a very small proportion of their total reserves in the form of gold. Developing countries have foregone enormous economic benefits as a result of their willingness to accept the pledge of the Bretton Woods system that the dollar was 'as good as gold'. Indeed, it will be shown that the creation and distribution of international reserves via gold revaluation has had the effect of depriving developing countries of reserves amounting to more than $100 billion.

Based on the quantitative results presented in this chapter, it will be argued that urgent attention should be given by the international community to the question of redressing the enormous inequities brought about in recent years by the *de facto* revaluation of reserve asset gold. In this context, it will be shown that a viable means for effecting such a redressment — and at the same time promoting a large-scale transfer of resources *to* developing countries — exists through the creation of a fund for development, based on official holdings of gold.

The outline of this chapter is as follows. The first section, which serves as background to the material presented in the remainder of the chapter, will contain a brief discussion of international reserve assets, paying particular attention to gold, Special Drawing Rights and related issues (e.g. the 'link'). The second section will consider the implications, in so far as developing countries are concerned, arising from the effective revaluation of gold reserves. Estimates will be provided both of the gains which have accrued to gold-holding countries as well as the reserves foregone by those low income countries which during the Bretton Woods system were encouraged to hold their reserves in a form other than gold. The third section will provide an historical perspective on the present distribution of reserve asset gold, and the fourth section will then examine the feasibility of establishing a 'Gold Account for Development' in order to partially counteract the inequities which have arisen. The chapter will close with a conclusion.

I   International reserves

The traditionally-cited 'international reserves' of a country consist of its holdings of four categories of reserve assets: gold, foreign exchange, Reserve Position in the International Monetary Fund (IMF) and Special Drawing Rights (SDRs). While the level of international reserves of a country should, in principle, indicate its international liquidity position, there are several important qualifications to this statement. To the extent that reserve *assets* have been built up by accruing reserve *liabilities* — for example, foreign exchange acquired by central bank swaps or through borrowing on the Eurocurrency market — such liabilities should be deducted to arrive at a more accurate pricture of the *net* reserve position of a country. In addition, regardless of the manner in which reserves are defined, they generally take no account of a country's potential borrowing capacity (e.g. on the Eurocurrency market).

The use of gold and foreign exchange as reserve assets in principle implies no future liabilities,[3] an increase in the valuation of either of these assets — arising from an increase in the price of gold or of a currency forming a part of the reserve portfolio — therefore has a *wealth* effect as well as a *liquidity* effect.

By contrast, the other two forms of reserve assets — Reserve Position in the IMF and SDRs — can be viewed as essentially representing potential borrowing rights. For most countries, the IMF Reserve Position is simply the amount which it can borrow unconditionally from the IMF under its first credit tranche[4] (formerly known as the gold tranche). Similarly, recent changes in the SDR have had the effect of transforming it from 'paper gold' to a credit facility; the implications of this will be explored later in this section of the chapter.

Gold and SDRs as international reserve assets

Throughout the early years of the Bretton Woods system, gold remained the dominant reserve asset. As late as 1967 reserve holdings of gold accounted for more than one-half of the total value of international reserves, and it was not until 1970 that gold was displaced by foreign exchange as the most important international reserve asset. Nevertheless, by the early 1960s it had become apparent that the growth in world trade, and the concomitant need for increased international reserves, was far larger than the rate at which gold was being added to the international monetary supply. The need for increased reserves was therefore being satisfied almost entirely by dollars from continuing US balance of payments deficits, and growing dissatisfaction with this emerging 'dollar exchange standard' led to considerable discussion during the 1960s of alternative means for providing sufficient international reserves in a controlled and rational manner.

Some, notably the French, argued for an increase in the official price of gold (which had remained unchanged at $35 per ounce since 1933) as a means for increasing the level of world reserves. This suggestion was decisively rejected, however, one of the principal objections being that it would lead to an inequitable distribution of new international liquidity. Thus, Otmar Emminger, subsequently President of the Deutsche Bundesbank, noted in 1967 that in the event of an increase in the official price of gold, 'countries that have relied on the U.S. pledge [to exchange dollars for gold at the "immutable" price of $35 per ounce] and have held a lower proportion of gold in their reserves would be penalized. Gold hoarders would be rewarded.'[5]

In 1967 agreement was reached on the creation of Special Drawing Rights as a new reserve asset, and in the intervening years there has been a growing consensus that the SDR should become the principal reserve asset of the international monetary system. Correspondingly, there has been agreement that the role of gold as a reserve asset should be progressively diminished. In June 1974 the Committee on Reform of the International Monetary System and Related Issues, generally known as the Committee of Twenty, issued its 'Outline of Reform': in so far as international reserve assets were concerned, it was stated that 'the SDR will become the principal reserve asset and the role of gold and of reserve currencies will be reduced'. This pledge was subsequently incorporated in the Second Amendment to the Articles of Agreement of the IMF, which was adopted in April 1978.[6]

The link

In the negotiations leading to the creation of the SDR, there was considerable debate as to whether the SDR should take the form of a wholly-owned reserve asset ('paper gold') or whether it should be simply a new borrowing facility within the IMF. In the end a compromise was struck: a 'restitution' requirement was established, whereby over any five-year period each country would be required to maintain on average 30 per cent of its cumulative allocations of SDRs. At the same time, the interest rate on the SDR – to be credited to countries holding more than their allocations and to be deducted from countries holding less – was set at 1.5 per cent, considerably below the prevailing market interest rate.

In this way the SDR represented neither paper gold nor a traditional borrowing facility. The 70 per cent not subject to restitution could in fact be considered as similar to paper gold, differing only in the regard that when used, an interest rate of 1.5 per cent would be charged; since there was no repayment obligation, the portion not subject to restitution could also be regarded as essentially representing the right to print (international) money or to issue a console (permanent bond) carrying the same interest rate. For the 30 per cent subject to restitution, the analogy would be to the right to borrow unconditionally for a fixed duration, with annual interest payments of 1.5 per cent.

In view of the minimal interest rate associated with the SDR as initially constituted, it was clear that the potential for associated resource transfers was large: recipients of SDR allocations would in effect be receiving long-term low-interest financial flows. As a result, a number of people — academic economists as well as spokesmen for developing countries — argued that the future creation of international liquidity should be *linked* to a transfer of resources to developing countries. Specifically, it was proposed that developing countries should receive a larger proportion of SDRs than would be dictated by their IMF quotas alone.

Despite widespread support for this idea, agreement was never reached on the 'link'. This was largely due to the opposition of several members of the Group of Ten, who argued that the international monetary system should be 'neutral' in so far as resource transfers were concerned. Nevertheless, interest in the 'link' has remained strong, and in the initial issue of this *Review*, Raul Prebisch, the first Secretary-General of UNCTAD, suggested that at 'an opportune moment, the idea of the link should be revived, its purpose being to channel resources towards development'.[7]

However, recent changes in the nature of the SDR which were designed to make it a more attractive reserve asset — specifically, the fact that it now carried a near-market rate of interest[8] — mean that the receipt of SDR allocations implies little (if any) command over real resources. Consequently, an SDR allocation can now be regarded as functionally equivalent to an interest subsidization scheme which allows the recipient to borrow at rates of interest only slightly lower than the market rate. Indeed, at the present time, the financial flow associated with an SDR allocation would not even qualify as 'concessional' assistance, using that term as it is conventionally defined.[9]

Gold and the IMF

Until the adoption of the Second Amendment to the Articles of Agreement of the IMF, member countries were required to pay one-quarter of their quotas in the form of gold. As a result, by the mid-1970s the IMF had become one of the largest official holders of gold reserves, second only to the US. In the 1976 Jamaica Agreement reached by the Interim Committee of the IMF, however, the role of gold in the Fund was effectively ended, and members were no longer required to provide gold to the Fund when quotas were increased. At the same time, agreement was also reached that approximately one-third of the IMF gold stock would be disposed of: 25 million ounces were to be sold to IMF members, in proportion to their quotas, at the nominal price of 35 SDR per ounce while a further 25 million ounces were to be sold at public auctions over a four-year period, with the profits going to a Trust Fund for the benefit of the poorer developing countries.

II   International reserves and the *de facto* revaluation of gold

A. The level and composition of international reserves

Despite what many thought was international agreement to progressively reduce the role of gold in the international monetary system, in recent years a number of events have shown that the world is moving increasingly in the direction of an enhanced role for gold as a result of the *de facto* revaluation of gold reserves. As a result, the 'effective' level of international reserves is both far greater than generally recognized and extremely sensitive to day-to-day fluctuations in the market price for gold. Such increases in the level of world reserves clearly bear little, if any, relationship to the increased value of world trade,[10] fail to take into account the variation in complementary supplies of international reserves (foreign exchange, SDR, etc.), and effectively frustrate attainment of the internationally agreed objective of bringing under control one of the most important variables in the international monetary system.

Table 5.1 provides information on the level and composition of international reserves in the 1970s. Gold reserves are valued at the end-year London market prices; for reference, the level of reserves when gold is valued at the former official price of 35 SDR per ounce is also shown.[11] One of the most striking facts to emerge from the table is that the value of world[12] reserves increased *ten-fold* during the decade of the 1970s, and has increased by a further 20 per cent in the first half of 1980 alone. This enormous growth in reserves has been accounted for almost entirely by increased holdings of foreign exchange (principally US dollars) and increased valuation of gold reserves, with the contribution of gold revaluation (62 per cent) being nearly twice that of foreign exchange (34 per cent). The rapid rise in the market price of gold in the late 1970s has effectively restored to gold its earlier role as the major international reserve asset, as by the end of 1979 it represented more than 60 per cent of the value of world reserves.

Largely as a result of this enormous, and unprecedented, growth in the effective level of world reserves, the repeated calls by spokesmen of developing countries for increased allocations of SDRs[13] have gone largely unheeded: allocations of SDRs have continued to be both infrequent and relatively small. Indeed, after the initial three-year programme of allocations totalling 13 billion SDRs ended in early 1972, there were no further allocations until 1979, when a new three-year programme, amounting to 12 billion SDRs, was begun.

The data presented in Table 5.1 show that SDR allocations have accounted for only 2 per cent of the growth in international reserves in the 1970s, or 6 per cent if gold is valued at 35 SDR per ounce. Consequently, as of 30 June 1980, world holdings of SDRs amounted to only $21 billion, barely *one-fiftieth* of the total value of international reserve assets. In contrast, since March 1979 the participating members in the European Monetary System have alone created more than $45 billion of *official* reserves through the exchange of members' gold reserves for European Currency Units.[14]

Table 5.1 The Level and Composition of International Reserves in the 1970s* (millions of US dollars and as per cent of total)

Type of reserve asset	1969	1970	1971	1972	1973	1974	1975	1976	1977	1978	1979	1980	Per cent increase 1969 to 1979 due to: Gold at 35 SDR per ounce price	Gold at market price
Total**	78,890	95,747	139,419	186,491	255,132	366,437	328,516	353,391	442,553	548,933	849,960	1,010,560	–	100.0
	100.0	100.0	100.0	100.0	100.0	100.0	100.0	100.0	100.0	100.0	100.0	100.0		
Foreign exchange	33,021	45,432	81,376	104,162	122,604	154,829	160,787	186,276	243,299	288,091	298,232	306,198	88.9	34.4
	41.9	47.5	58.4	55.9	48.1	42.3	48.9	52.7	55.0	52.5	35.1	30.3		
IMF reserve position	6,726	7,697	6,895	6,867	7,441	10,829	14,778	20,606	21,973	19,332	15,492	16,454	2.9	1.1
	8.5	8.0	4.9	3.7	2.9	3.0	4.5	5.8	5.0	3.5	1.8	1.6		
SDRs	–	3,124	6,379	9,430	10,624	10,845	10,260	10,056	9,879	10,566	16,439	21,267	5.5	2.1
	–	3.3	4.6	5.1	4.2	3.0	3.1	2.8	2.2	1.9	1.9	2.1		
Gold*	39,143	39,494	44,769	66,032	114,463	189,933	142,692	136,453	167,403	230,944	519,797	666,641	–	62.3
	49.6	41.2	32.1	35.4	44.9	51.8	43.4	38.6	37.8	42.1	61.2	66.0		
For reference: gold valued at 35 SDR per ounce														
Total	78,670	93,243	133,643	159,119	183,723	220,144	227,511	258,116	318,296	364,584	376,971	391,204	100.0	–
	100.0	100.0	100.0	100.0	100.0	100.0	100.0	100.0	100.0	100.0	100.0	100.0		
Gold	38,923	36,990	38,993	38,660	43,055	43,641	41,686	41,178	43,146	46,596	46,809	47,285	2.6	–
	49.5	39.7	29.2	24.3	23.4	19.8	18.3	16.0	13.6	12.8	12.4	12.1		

* Reserve figures are end-year except for 1980; for 1980 as of 30 June.

** With gold valued at market price, as reported by the IMF. EEC data have been adjusted to reflect uniform valuation of gold at 35 SDR per ounce, including gold held by the European Monetary Cooperation Fund.

Source: Calculations based on information presented in *International Financial Statistics* (Washington, DC: IMF, various issues).

B. Implications for developing countries

At a time when the large majority of countries are beset with severe economic problems, the increase in the value of world reserve assets by $650 billion in the past three and a half years may well serve to 'fuel the fires' of inflation. Indeed, one noted observer of the international monetary system, Robert Triffin, has recently stated that the 'bookkeeping profits' arising from gold revaluation will 'be passed on sooner or later to Governments, and are practically certain to elicit in many countries more expansionist fiscal and monetary policies *in the future* than would have been the case otherwise'.[15]

To the extent that such expansionist policies exacerbate the level of international inflation, real costs will be imposed on developing countries in the form of higher import prices. Nevertheless, for developing countries the most important implications arising from the effective revaluation of reserve asset gold follow directly from the fact that, when dollar convertibility into gold was ended, the distribution of gold reserves was highly uneven, even in comparison with the relatively low levels of their quotas in the IMF.

Table 5.2 presents information on current holdings of reserve asset gold by principal economic groups[16] as well as by major individual gold-holding countries. From this it can be seen that of the total volume of reserve asset gold held by individual countries (i.e. slightly more than 1 billion ounces[17]), 90 per cent is held by the central banks of developed market economy countries, 6 per cent by those of non-oil exporting developing countries and 4 per cent by oil-exporting developing countries. Moreover, nearly three-quarters of world reserve asset gold is held by seven countries — US, Federal Republic of Germany, France, Italy, Switzerland, Netherlands and Belgium — five of which individually possess a larger amount than all non-oil exporting developing countries combined.

As stated earlier, an increase in the valuation of gold reserves represents a potential transfer of resources, since (unlike SDR allocations or IMF drawings) there is no off-setting liability. In order to gain an approximation of the

Table 5.2   The distribution of reserve asset gold and the gains from gold revaluation in the 1970s

Country or country grouping	Quantity* (million ounces)	Share (per cent)	Value at market price* (million US dollars)	Gross gains** (million US dollars)	Net gains*** (Million US dollars)	Per capita US dollars
World	1,015.23	100.0	519,797	484,265	459,054	155
Developed Market Economy	916.81	90.3	469,407	437,318	414,501	521
of which:						
US	264.60	26.1	135,475	126,214	121,806	553
Germany, Fed. Rep. of	118.98	11.7	60,918	56,753	53,268	868
France	102.32	10.1	52,388	48,807	45,812	857
Italy	83.34	8.2	42,670	39,753	37,313	656
Switzerland	83.28	8.2	42,639	39,725	37,273	5,888
Netherlands	54.93	5.4	28,124	26,202	24,592	1,753
Belgium–Luxembourg	42.73	4.2	21,878	20,382	19,132	1,938
Total above	750.18	73.9	384,092	357,836	339,196	803
Developing	98.42	9.7	50,391	46,946	44,553	21
of which:						
Oil exporting	37.18	3.7	19,036	17,735	16,657	49
Non-oil exporting	61.24	6.0	31,355	29,211	27,896	15
of which:						
Most seriously affected	16.19	1.6	8,289	7,723	7,271	6
Least developed	1.64	0.2	840	782	740	3

* As of 31 December 1979; for EEC countries, figures include the 20 per cent of their gold stock held by EMCF.
** Gross appreciation in value of end-1979 gold reserves during the period 31 December 1969 to 31 December 1979.
*** Gross gains net of interest earnings foregone, which have been calculated under the assumption that reserves would have been held in dollars and invested in US Treasury short-term notes. The net gains also incorporate adjustments to reflect changes in gold stocks during the course of the decade.
Source: Calculations based on information presented in *International Financial Statistics* (Washington, DC: IMF, various issues).

'wealth' effect' which has been conferred on holders of reserve asset gold, Table 5.2 also provides information on the gains, both 'gross' and 'net', which have accrued to holders of reserve asset gold in the 1970s. The gross gains represent the difference between the present (market) valuation of a country's gold reserves and the valuation which would have prevailed at the beginning of the decade (i.e. when gold was officially valued at $35 per ounce). The present valuation refers to that of 31 December 1979, when gold was valued at $512 per ounce, considerably less than the market price of gold which prevailed during the first six months of 1980.

Defined in this manner, the 'gross' gains make no allowance for the opportunity costs associated with holding gold reserves, namely the interest receipts foregone by not holding interest-earning foreign exchange reserves. On the other hand, since the gains refer to the appreciation in the value of gold held as reserves by individual countries at the end of 1979, they do not fully reflect the profits received by several countries which sold substantial amounts of gold at market prices during the course of the decade.[18] The *net* gains from gold revaluation therefore incorporate adjustments for both interest earnings foregone[19] and profits from sales (and purchases[20]) of gold reserves at market prices.

To a certain extent, the gains accruing to gold-holding countries can be regarded as 'paper' profits, for if such countries were *simultaneously* to attempt to fully realize these gains by selling their gold stock, they would inevitably drive down the price of gold. Nevertheless, the growing recognition of the appropriateness of a market valuation for gold reserves has been highlighted by the recently issued 1980 edition of the World Bank *World Development Report*, which for the first time values the gold reserves of *all* countries at their market valuation.[21]

Bearing these comments in mind, the results portrayed in Table 5.2 are none the less striking: the increase in the effective value of international reserves that has resulted from the market revaluation of gold is both of an enormous magnitude and distributed in a highly skewed fashion. For the developed countries as a whole, their gross gains during the 1970s from the *de facto* revaluation of reserve asset gold amount to the staggering figure of $437 billion. Even after deducting the interest earnings foregone, the net gains by these same countries still amount to $415 billion. By contrast, the gains accruing to developing countries have been of a far more modest nature, namely 10 per cent of the world total — corresponding to their share in world gold reserves. Only 6 per cent of the net gains have gone to the non-oil exporting developing countries, while the Most Seriously Affected (MSA) and the Least Developed Countries, two groups identified by the General Assembly of the United Nations as meriting special assistance, have received 1.6 per cent and 0.16 per cent, respectively, of the overall gains from gold revaluation.[22]

Viewed on a *per capita* basis, the disparity in the gains received by different groups assumes even greater proportions. The 'windfall' gain received by residents of developed market economy countries amounts to more than $500 per person; in the seven principal gold-holding countries the net gains range frome a 'low' of $553 per person (US) to nearly $6,000 per person (Switzerland). In contrast, for the non-oil exporting developing countries, the *per capita* net increase in gold reserves has amounted to only $15, while the corresponding figures for the MSA and the Least Developed Countries are $6 and $2.80, respectively.

To this stage, the discussion has focused on the *wealth* effects (i.e. the potential for resource transfers) associated with the effective revaluation of reserve asset gold. A somewhat different perspective can be obtained by examining the *liquidity* effects of gold revaluation. Despite international agreement that the SDR would become the 'principal reserve asset' of the international monetary system — and that the role of gold would be progressively reduced — more than three-fifths of reserve growth in the 1970s took the form of increased valuation of gold reserves. Developing countries might well wish to enquire what their international liquidity positions would be today if this massive reserve growth had occurred instead via increased allocations of SDRs. While, as noted earlier, the resource transfers associated with SDR allocations are relatively small, increased allocations of SDRs would none the less have represented an important source of international liquidity — available at relatively low rates of interest — for the large majority of developing countries which have only limited (if any) access to international capital markets.[23]

In order to quantify the reserves (i.e. SDRs) foregone by developing countries from gold revaluation, it has been hypothesized that the net increase during the 1970s in the effective value of gold reserves attributable to market revaluation of gold — i.e. $459.1 billion — had occurred instead through increased allocations of SDRs.[24] To the extent that the increase in the gold reserves of an individual country due to gold revaluation is less than the amount of SDRs it would have received via increased allocations of SDRs, the difference can be denoted as the reserves 'foregone' by that country.[25] Conversely, to the extent that a country's gold reserves have increased by more than what it would have received via SDR allocations, the difference represents that country's 'excess' reserve gains from gold revaluation. By making such comparisons, light will be shed on the relative advantages for developing countries of an international monetary system whose reserve growth is based on SDR allocations, as compared to the present system in which reserve growth has become increasingly dependent on the market price for gold.

Viewed in this context, it is clear that even in the absence of an SDR 'link', the non-oil exporting developing countries could have anticipated receiving 22 per cent of the increase in international reserves in the 1970s, i.e. a proportion equal to their combined share in IMF quotas. Their claim to this share in increased reserves arising from gold revaluation is considerably strengthened by the fact that over the course of the decade these countries accounted for virtually the same proportion of the increased value in world reserves, if the increase due to gold revaluation is excluded.

Table 5.3 shows that at the end of 1979, the level of international reserves of developing countries would have been $103 billion larger than their actual level, if world reserves had increased through further allocations of SDRs rather than through a revaluation of reserve asset gold. For the non-oil exporting developing countries, the reserves

Table 5.3 Value of reserves gained and foregone due to gold revaluation, as compared to equivalent SDR allocations, in the 1970s

Country or country grouping	Share of IMF quota (per cent)	Net gains from hypothetical SDR allocations (million of US dollars)	Net gains from gold revalaution* (million of US dollars)	Net reserves gained or foregone** (million of US dollars)
World	100.0	459,054	459,054	0
Developed market economy of which:	67.8	311,178	414,501	103,323
US	21.5	98,890	121,806	22,916
Germany, Fed. Rep. of	5.5	25,367	53,268	27,901
Italy	3.2	14,589	37,313	22,724
Switzerland	–	–	37,273	37,273
Netherlands	2.4	11,154	24,592	13,438
Belgium–Luxembourg	2.4	10,836	19,132	8,296
Total above	40.0	183,414	339,196	155,782
Developing of which:	32.2	147,876	44,553	–103,323
Oil exporting	10.2	46,921	16,657	–30,264
Non-oil exporting	22.0	100,955	27,896	–73,059
Most seriously affected	8.2	37,849	7,271	–30,578
Least developed	2.0	9,368	740	–8,628

* See Table 5.2.
** Net reserves gained or foregone are defined as the difference between the net gains from gold revaluation and the increase in reserves which would have occurred if an equivalent amount of international reserves (i.e. SDRs) had been created and distributed according to IMF quotas.
Source: Calculations based on information presented in *International Financial Statistics* (Washington, DC: IMF, various issues).

'foregone' through gold revaluation in the 1970s were $73 billion, an amount nearly equal to their actual reserve holdings at the end of 1979. For the MSA and the Least Developed Countries, the reserves 'foregone' during the 1970s amounted to $31 billion and $8.6 billion, respectively; for each of these two groups of countries, their 'hypothetical' reserves at the end of 1979 were considerably more than twice the actual level.

Also apparent from Table 5.3 is the extent to which the seven principal gold-holding countries have received reserves far in excess of those which would have resulted if the increased world liquidity due to gold revaluation had been distributed instead as SDRs in accordance with IMF quotas. While developed market economy countries as a group received excess reserves of $103 billion (the counterpart to the reserves foregone by developing countries), these seven countries collectively received excess reserves of more than $155 billion.[26]

III The historical pattern of reserve accumulation in the Bretton Woods era

Developing countries have undoubtedly come to regret deeply the fact that, unlike a number of the industrialized countries, they chose (indeed, were encouraged) to build up their reserve positions in the 1950s and 1960s through acquisitions of foreign exchange instead of through increased holdings of gold. To provide some historical perspective on the evolution of the distribution of reserve asset gold in the Bretton Woods era, the reserve growth of the non-oil exporting developing countries has been compared to that experienced by five of the principal gold-holding countries: Belgium, France, Federal Republic of Germany, Italy and the Netherlands.[27] The results are presented in Table 5.4.

What emerges clearly from the table is that at the end of the 1940s, the non-oil exporting developing countries owned virtually the same amount of gold reserves as did Belgium, France, Federal Republic of Germany, Italy and the Netherlands combined. Over the course of the succeeding two decades, however, more than two-thirds of the growth in

Table 5.4 The relative importance of gold as a reserve asset: developing and selected developed market economy countries, 1949 and 1969

Country or country grouping	Reserve asset gold holdings (million ounces)		Percentage of reserve growth 1949–1969 due to:			Gold as percentage of total reserves (end-year 1969)
	1949	1969	Gold	Foreign exchange	IMF reserve	
Developed Market Economy						
Belgium–Luxembourg	20.00	43.40	58.2	33.3	8.5	63.6
France	15.51	101.34	92.3	7.7	0.0	92.5
Germany, Fed. Rep. of	0.00	116.56	58.8	36.8	4.4	57.2
Italy	7.31	84.46	62.5	17.6	20.0	58.6
Netherlands	5.73	49.16	71.1	8.4	20.5	68.0
Total above	48.55	394.92	67.1	23.3	9.5	66.1
Developing						
Total	67.85	97.78	13.5	79.2	7.3	21.4
Oil exporting	20.50	37.44	19.4	75.1	5.5	30.5
Non-oil exporting	47.35	60.34	9.7	81.9	8.4	18.0

* Data refer to end-year 1949 and 1969.
Source: Calculations based on information presented in *International Financial Statistics* (Washington, DC: IMF, various issues).

international reserves in these five countries was accounted for by increased holdings of gold. On the other hand, the severe liquidity constraints facing the large majority of developing countries meant that these countries could ill-afford to forego the interest (albeit modest) earned on foreign exchange holdings in order to speculate on a future revaluation of gold reserves. For the poorer countries, growth in international reserves was therefore concentrated largely in foreign exchange reserves: indeed, for the non-oil export-ing developing countries, less than 10 per cent of reserve growth took the form of increased holdings of gold.

Table 5.4 shows that at the end of the 1960s, nearly two-thirds of the total international reserve assets held by these five developed market economy countries were in the form of gold, while for the non-oil exporting developing countries the share of gold in total reserves was less than one-fifth. As a result, the gold reserves held by these five countries — which 20 years earlier had been virtually the same as those held by the non-oil exporting developing countries — were now larger by a factor of more than six.

The vast disparity between the gains received from gold revaluation by these five countries ($180 billion according to Table 5.2) and those received by the non-oil exporting developing countries ($28 billion) is attributable in large part to their disparate patterns of reserve accumulation in the 1950s and 1960s.[28] If the non-oil exporting developing coun-tries had chosen to hold the same proportion of their inter-national reserves in gold as was the case for these five gold-accumulating countries (66.1 per cent), the gold reserves of the non-oil exporting developing countries at the end of the 1960s would have been 222 million ounces, as compared with their actual gold holdings of 60 million ounces. Valued at the June 1980 market price, this 'extra' gold — 162 million ounces — would today be worth more than $100 billion.

Viewed in this context, it is clear that developing coun-tries have paid a heavy price for their willingness to abide by the rules of the Bretton Woods system and to accept the pledge of the US that the dollar was 'as good as gold'. These countries might well ask why some of the major beneficiaries of the current *de facto* revaluation of gold reserves are precisely those countries which, by requiring the US to convert their dollar holdings into gold, put such a heavy burden on the international monetary system in the 1960s and early 1970s.[29]

IV   A gold account for development

Based on the quantitative results presented in this chapter, it is clear that developing countries in general, and the non-oil exporting developing countries in particular, have strong grounds for asserting that the international monetary system has been far from 'neutral' in its distribution of international liquidity. Indeed, in view of the present international support for a massive transfer of resources to stimulate economic growth in the developing countries, it seems increasingly ironic that one of the largest potential resource transfers in history has recently occurred, not in favour of the poorer developing countries, but in favour of the wealthiest of the industrialized countries.

In this connection, a particularly ironic note is struck by the fact that, despite widespread agreement that flows of official development assistance to developing countries should attain the level of 0.7 per cent of GNP, the level actually reached in 1979 by the developed market economy countries was the same as in 1970, i.e. 0.34 per cent of GNP, or less than one-half of the target stipulated by the United Nations. During the 1970s, the total value of official development assistance provided by developed market economy countries amounted to approximately $125 billion, less than one-third of the net gains realized by these countries over the same period of time from the *de facto* market revaluation of reserve asset gold.

The unwillingness of developed market economy countries to significantly increase their concessional financial flows to developing countries appears especially untimely in the light of the precarious economic situation currently facing the majority of developing countries. Reports recently issued by both the World Bank and the IMF have indicated that the adjustment problems which will confront the developing countries in the 1980s will be particularly serious ones and are likely to be compounded by a shortage of long-term financing.[30]

For this reason, it seems imperative that the international community give urgent consideration to redressing the present inequities which have arisen from the massive revaluation of gold reserves. Perhaps the most obvious means of doing so would be through the imposition of a tax on the 'excess profits' of the major gold-holding countries and the distribution of the proceeds to countries holding only a small proportion of their reserves in the form of gold. This would allow a more equitable distribution of the massive gains from gold revaluation than those which have arisen under the status quo. Indeed, a number of the suggestions in the 1960s to increase the price of gold were accompanied by proposals to redistribute a portion of the gains to the non gold-holding countries. While the precise amount of a gold tax would have to be the subject of detailed negotiations, the quantitative results cited earlier strongly suggest that in order to significantly counteract the inequities which have arisen, such a tax would have to amount to at least 10–15 per cent of the reserve gold holdings of the developed market economy countries.

To take effect, such a plan would clearly require the unanimous consent of the major gold-holding countries. The achievement of such a consensus is extremely unlikely, however, especially as several of these countries (e.g. France, Italy, Netherlands and the UK) have already officially revalued their gold reserves at the market price. Moreover, given the fact that legislatures in a number of developed market economy countries have been unwilling, or unable, to approve legislation to substantially increase their flows of development assistance to developing countries, the prospects for simultaneous legislative approval in these countries of such a potentially controversial measure as a 'Gold Account for Development' would seem quite remote.[31]

There exists, however, an alternative course of action whose implementation would be far easier to achieve – namely, the creation of a gold account for development based on the remaining gold stock held by the IMF. As discussed earlier, the more than 100 million ounces of gold still held by the IMF[32] no longer have any official role in the Fund, and in principle there is no obstacle, legal or otherwise, to its use as the basis for a 'Gold Account for Development'.[33] Indeed, in addition to the disposal of one-third of the IMF gold stock in the last four years, its availability for 'other' purposes was highlighted earlier this year during the discussions of the ill-fated 'Substitution Account', in which it was proposed that a portion of the remaining IMF gold stock could be used to provide the necessary guarantee against exchange risk.[34]

In establishing a gold account for development on the basis of the IMF gold stock, a number of practical questions would have to be resolved, including the list of countries eligible to benefit from the resources of the account. A more fundamental question relates to the appropriate manner in which the resources of the gold account would be distributed to eligible countries. Here at least two different approaches could be envisaged, analogous to the two ways in which one-third of the IMF gold stock has already been disposed of.[35]

The more direct way would involve 'selling' the gold to qualifying developing countries, in agreed amounts, for the nominal price of 35 SDR per ounce. Individual recipient countries would then be free to use the gold for any purpose they wished: undoubtedly some would seek to sell their gold and use the profits to effect an immediate transfer of resources, while others might choose to hold it in anticipation of a future appreciation in market value. In the latter case, the country would none the less derive immediate benefits from its enhanced creditworthiness,[36] including the possibility of using the gold, valued at a market price, as collateral for loans.

The second means whereby the IMF gold stock could be mobilized in the service of developing countries would be through the creation of an enlarged 'trust fund' analogous to that currently in operation under the auspices of the IMF. The 103 million ounces of gold held by the IMF could be auctioned off at regular intervals, with the 'profits'[37] placed in a fund for development to be used for making low-interest loans (or grants) to eligible developing countries. It is clear, however, that the sale of the remaining IMF gold stock over a short period of time would reduce the potential for effecting resource transfers to developing countries by driving down the price of gold. Nevertheless, the experiences of both the IMF and the US gold-sales programmes suggest that sales of this magnitude over a protracted period of 10 or more years would not unduly depress the market price of gold.[38] In the interim, the development account could utilize that portion of the gold not yet sold as collateral to secure low-interest loans from the private capital market.

As of 30 June 1980 the bookkeeping value of the IMF gold stock was $4.8 billion, while its market value was $67.6 billion. The initial capital value of a gold account for development established at this time would therefore have been $62.8 billion. Viewed in the context of the earlier discussions of both the reserves foregone by the non-oil exporting developing countries — more than $73 billion in the 1970s[39] — and the massive profits which have accrued to the developed market economy countries — whose combined gold reserves are nine times those of the IMF — it is clear that the resources of such a development account are by no means excessive.

Regardless of the approach employed, the establishment of a gold account based on the IMF gold stock would result in a significant transfer of resources to developing countries in the years to come, and would at least partially counteract the reserve transfer of resources associated with the recent revaluation of gold reserves. This would appear particularly appropriate in view of the long-standing commitments of the developed market economy countries to significantly increase their resource transfers to developing countries, and their equally long-term failure to meet the aid targets established by the United Nations.

Conclusion

This chapter has shown that developing countries, whose effective input into decisions concerning the international monetary system has been minimal, have foregone enormous reserve asset holdings in recent years as a result of a major change in the international monetary system — namely, the *de facto* revaluation of reserve asset gold. The quantitative evidence presented in this chapter clearly demonstrates that an SDR-based international monetary system, even without a link to development assistance, is far more in the interest of developing countries than the currently emerging system, which is based increasingly on a market valuation of reserve asset gold.

Not only has the international monetary system been evolving for some years in a highly unstructured manner, but it has become increasingly apparent that no reform of a global nature will be forthcoming in the near future. Given this state of affairs, it is certainly in the interest of the developing countries to press for a redressment of some of the major inequities which have arisen from the *de facto* revaluation of reserve asset gold, even in the absence of any overall agreement on the precise nature of the post-Bretton Woods international monetary system.

Indeed, a discussion of the issues raised in this chapter is especially appropriate at the present time. The Eleventh Special Session of the General Assembly of the United Nations has recently met to discuss the appropriate strategy for the Third International Development Decade. The ensuing Conference on Global Negotiations, which is to be held in 1981* under UN auspices, would appear to provide an ideal forum for developing countries to voice their legitimate grievances concerning the massive *reverse* transfer of resources arising from the revaluation of gold reserves, and to press their case for the establishment of a gold account for development, based on the gold reserves held by the IMF.

In recent years there have been a number of proposals for the creation of a special 'fund for development' to accelerate the development of the poorer countries.[40] The failure to reach agreement on the establishment of such a development fund has in most cases been due to the difficulty in providing a compelling rationale as to the equity of the resulting resource transfers or a convincing demonstration of the feasibility of the proposals.

In so far as a gold account for development is concerned,

*This was held in August/September 1981 in New York, but proved to be inconclusive on all issues. Efforts are under way to resume the Global Negotiations in April 1982.

this chapter has shown that the case on equity grounds for a transfer of resources to developing countries, based on IMF gold holdings, is an overwhelming one. Massive profits have accrued in recent years to those countries which during the 1950s and 1960s pursued a policy of converting foreign exchange holdings into gold, or whose currencies historically served as reserve assets.[41] In contrast, developing countries, which throughout the Bretton Woods era were discouraged from building up their reserve asset holdings of gold, have received an inordinately small share of the gains from gold revaluation.

Of equal importance to the equity argument, however, is the fact that the proposals advanced in this chapter for the establishment of a development account based on IMF gold reserves are entirely practical. In particular, it should be emphasized that the difference between the current market valuation of the IMF gold stock and its book value (i.e. with gold valued at 35 SDR per ounce) is a 'good' which at present belongs to no one. Its distribution to developing countries — either directly or through the creation of an enlarged trust fund   would therefore be a costless one, for it would impose no direct burden on the IMF or on any single country.

Indeed, a decision will eventually have to be taken concerning the disposition of the 'bookkeeping' profits associated with the IMF gold stock, and such a decision will necessarily be a subjective one. The demonstrated need of developing countries for increased financial resource transfers, combined with the manner in which they have been discriminated against by the non-neutrality of the international monetary system, would therefore appear to offer irrefutable arguments for allowing these countries to share in this manner in the gains which have arisen from the market revaluation of gold reserves.

Notes

1 Either 35 SDR per ounce (the official price set by the IMF), $35 per ounce (the official price which had prevailed from 1933 to December 1971), or $42.22 per ounce (the official price which temporarily prevailed following the second US devaluation in February 1973).

2 In a recent article, it was shown that well over two-thirds of world

reserve asset gold is held by countries which have either officially revalued their gold reserves at a market-related price or have acted in a manner consistent with a market revaluation (e.g. by selling significant quantities of gold at market prices). See David A. Brodsky and Gary P. Sampson, 'The Value of Gold as a Reserve Asset', *World Development*, vol. 8, no. 3, March 1980, pp. 175-92.

3 Though, as noted above, in many cases foreign exchange holdings are acquired in a manner which simultaneously increases the reserve liabilities of a country.

4 A country also acquires an increased IMF Reserve Position whenever another member draws its currency from the Fund. In addition, the amount of a country's lending to the IMF (e.g. through the General Arrangements to Borrow, the Oil Facility and the Supplementary Financing Facility) is added to its Reserve Position.

5 Quoted in Randall Hinshaw, ed., *Monetary Reform and the Price of Gold*, Johns Hopkins University Press, Baltimore, 1967, p. 106.

6 Article VIII, Section 7 and Article XXII.

7 Similarly, the 'Outline for a Program of Action on International Monetary Reform' (also known as the 'Blue Book') prepared by the Group of Twenty-four in September 1979, and subsequently endorsed by the Group of Seventy-seven, calls for the 'early establishment of a link between SDR allocations and additional development assistance' and notes that 'the creation of such a link is long overdue' (A/C.2/34/13).

8 In 1979 the rate of interest charged for SDR use was raised to 80 per cent of the (weighted-average) market interest rate of the five major currencies in the SDR basket, while holders of SDRs now receive 72 per cent of the market rate. At the same time, the restitution requirement was reduced from 30 to 15 per cent. See IMF, *Annual Report 1979*, Washington, DC, pp. 65-7.

9 Concessional assistance as defined by the Development Assistance Committee (DAC) of the OECD consists of any financial flow whose associated *grant element* is at least 25 per cent. Over the period January to September 1980, the rate of interest associated with SDR use ranged from 8.25 per cent to 10.25 per cent, corresponding to grant elements from 17.5 per cent to *minus* 2.5 per cent.

10 For a comparison of recent growth in the level of international reserves with that of the value of world trade, see Brodsky and Sampson, op. cit., Table 3.

11 Following the US devaluation in December 1971, when the value of the SDR was raised from $1 to $1.08571, the official price of

gold remained 35 SDR per ounce. Since the Jamaica Agreement in January 1976, there has been no 'official' price for gold reserves.

12   For the purposes of this chapter, 'world' excludes the socialist countries of Eastern Europe and Asia, for which the relevant data are not available.

13   For example, in their 'Blue Book' on International Monetary Reform (op. cit.), the Group of Twenty-four called for 'an increase in the present agreed SDR allocations to meet the current difficult economic conditions' and 'regular annual allocations of SDRs, in amounts adequate to members' needs for reserve increases'.

14   In March 1979 (July 1979 for the UK) the members of the European Economic Community transferred 20 per cent of their reserve holdings of gold, valued at a market-related price, to the European Monetary Cooperation Fund in return for an allocation of ECUs. For a discussion of the implications of this massive expansion of European liquidity, see David Marsh, 'Battle Looms for the Gold in Europe's Budding Central Bank', *Financial Times*, 15 August 1980, p. 2.

15   'The Future of the International Monetary System', *Banca Nazionale del Lavoro Quarterly Review*, no. 132, March 1980, p. 33 (italics in the original).

16   The economic groups are as defined in the 1979 edition of the *UNCTAD Handbook of International Trade and Development Statistics.*

17   Including the 85 million ounces of EEC gold held by the European Monetary Cooperation Fund.

18   Estimated sales of gold reserves (in millions of ounces, and average price per ounce) since the second US devaluation in February 1973 have been by: US (17.0, $254), Portugal (5.5, $170), Mexico (3.7, $125) and Zaïre (1.2, $160). IMF, *International Financial Statistics* and *Balance of Payments Yearbook*, various issues.

19   Statistics published by the IMF indicate that throughout the 1970s nearly 80 per cent of foreign exchange reserves were held in the form of US dollars (IMF, *Annual Report 1979*, Washington, DC, p. 59). Hence, interest earnings foregone have been calculated on the assumption that reserves would have been held in US dollars and invested in US Treasury short-term notes.

20   Purchases of gold reserves by central banks of individual countries at market prices during the 1970s were negligible (less than 5 million ounces). Indeed, until the adoption of the Second Amendment to the Articles of Agreement of the IMF in 1978, IMF members were prohibited from purchasing gold at a price above the 'official' price (Article IV, Section 2).

21   Moreover, the argument against a market valuation of gold reserves can be applied equally well to the valuation of stocks of *any* commodity customarily valued at a market price; specifically, to the valuation of foreign exchange, which as a reserve asset is generally valued at its 'market' price (i.e. the exchange rate).

22   India holds more than one-half of the combined gold stock of the 45 MSA countries, while 60 per cent of the reserve asset gold of the 31 Least Developed Countries is held by Afghanistan.

23   For the non-oil exporting developing countries, nearly 90 per cent of all borrowing from the international capital market (i.e. bonds and Eurocurrency credits) in 1979 went to eleven countries, all (except Philippines) having *per capita* incomes in excess of $1,100. World Bank, *Borrowing in International Capital Markets*, EC-181/794 and *World Development Report 1980*.

24   In a recent paper (Brodsky and Sampson, op. cit.), three alternative frameworks for evaluating reserve losses were discussed. The framework presented here is an up-dated version of the second of these.

25   It should be emphasized that this exercise is concerned only with the *liquidity* effects of gold revaluation, for it assumes that individual countries would be indifferent to the choice between gold and SDRs. In view of the high interest rate currently associated with SDR use, it is clear that an increase in the value of a country's gold reserves imparts to it a far greater wealth effect than would an equivalent allocation of SDRs.

26   With reference to Table 5.3, it should be noted that Switzerland is not a member of the IMF and therefore receives no allocations of SDRs.

27   These five countries were chosen since among all IMF members they had the largest increase in gold reserves over the period under review.

28   It must be noted, of course, that these gold accumulating countries paid a price for their attachment to gold – i.e. the interest earnings foregone in the 1950s and 1960s from not holding interest-bearing foreign exchange reserves. Such foregone earnings – less than $15 billion – pale into insigificance, however, in comparison with the (net) gains realized by these countries in the 1970s (see Table 5.2).

29   Indeed, John Williamson has gone so far as to assert that 'as part of a systematic policy of making the gold exchange standard unworkable [France] initiated regular and substantial conversions of dollars into gold'. *The Failure of World Monetary Reform, 1971-1974*, Thomas Nelson, Middlesex, 1977, pp. 20-1. See also the quotation by Otmar Emminger, cited in Section I.

30   World Bank, *World Development Report 1980,* and International

Monetary Fund, *World Economic Outlook*, 1980, Washington, DC.

31 In this connection, one should note that the recently adopted platform of one of the two major political parties has been interpreted by many as calling for a restoration of the gold standard (*International Herald Tribune*, 1 August 1980, p. 3). See also the discussion of a return to the gold standard in 'Bring Back the Gold Standard?', *Dun's Review*, vol. 115, no. 4, April 1980, pp. 58–67.

32 As of 30 June 1980 the gold reserves of the IMF were 103.4 million ounces.

33 A decision to use the IMF gold stock in the manner proposed here could probably be done within the existing Articles of Agreement of the Fund (Article V, Section 12), although adoption of a new amendment might be necessary. In either case, approval of IMF members constituting 85 per cent of total quotas would be required; hence, the only individual country with the power to veto such a proposal would be the US.

34 See, for example, *IMF Survey*, 3 March 1980.

35 A second analogy is to the discussions on the appropriate means for distributing the additional liquidity which would have resulted from the implementation of the 'link'. Some argued that the additional SDRs should go directly to developing countries, while others recommended that they be channelled via multilateral institutions.

36 For example, in the case of the US, Triffin (op. cit., p. 43) has noted that US gold holdings are 'relevant . . . as one of the many reassurances to prospective creditors about our solvency, and as an indication of our ability to transfer gold at . . . market prices'.

37 That is, the difference between the sale price of IMF gold and its bookkeeping value of 35 SDR per ounce.

38 In 1979, for example, the London gold price rose from $226 per ounce to $512 per ounce, despite the US having sold more than 13 million ounces of gold.

39 The analysis presented in Section II was based on the end-1979 gold market price of $512 per ounce. Using the June 1980 market price of $653.50 per ounce would raise the level of reserves foregone by the non-oil exporting developing countries to more than $95 billion.

40 The proposed sources of revenue for such funds have been quite diverse: for example, international income taxes, levies on world trade and taxes on tourism.

41 In addition to holders of reserve asset gold, other large beneficiaries have been the major gold-producing nations, chiefly South Africa and the USSR.

6 MASSIVE TRANSFERS OF RESOURCES: MECHANISMS AND INSTITUTIONS

Michael Stewart*

I Introduction

This chapter takes as axiomatic the need for a substantially increased transfer of resources from the North to the South. The focus is on the transfer of financial resources which can directly or indirectly be used by the South to purchase goods and services from the North — or from other countries in the South — rather than on the transfer of goods as such (as in the case of food aid) or the provision of technical assistance. Although in some cases it is not practicable to discuss mechanisms in isolation from the institutions through which they would work, the basic plan of the chapter is to consider first the various mechanisms which it has been suggested would encourage such transfers to take place, and then to examine the role which existing and new institutions might play in the operation of these mechanisms.

II Mechanisms

ODA

From the point of view of developing countries, the best mechanism for the transfer of resources is Official Development Assistance (ODA) which takes the form of grants or loans on highly concessional terms. But although the developed countries as a whole are currently contributing no more than about half the target figure of 0.7 per cent of GNP to ODA, the prospects of any substantial increase in

* Lecturer at University College London, December 1980.

this percentage are bleak. Partly because most OECD countries are running balance of payments deficits, but mainly because tight controls on public expenditure are very widely regarded as a crucial element in anti-inflationary policies, there is little disposition in the North to increase, or in some cases even maintain, real levels of development assistance. Although in recent years OPEC countries have been contributing a significantly larger proportion of their GNP in aid than OECD countries, and may continue to do so, OPEC aid expenditures still constitute a relatively small proportion of the total, and are unlikely to alter the general picture of a rise in total ODA over the next few years on a scale too small to make any significant contribution to the South's need for additional resources. Nevertheless, such additional flows of ODA as do become available can be of great importance, for example when used to subsidize the cost of non-concessional resource transfers to poorer borrowers. A number of the mechanisms discussed below are dependent on such subsidies, whether financed by ODA or in other ways.

A Medium-term Facility

One mechanism which has been proposed for transferring resources is the establishment of a Medium-term Facility in the IMF.[1] Such a facility would enable developing countries to adjust more gradually than is permitted under present Fund procedures to structural balance of payments problems which have arisen through factors outside their control, and thus avoid or minimize cuts in imports which would adversely affect both their own development programme and the course of world trade. Drawings on the new facility would be on first credit tranche conditions (as was the case with the Oil Facility introduced in 1974), so that countries would be required by the Fund to do no more than make reasonable efforts to solve their structural balance of payments problem in a way that did not disrupt their development programme. Repayments of drawings would not need to be completed until 10 years after the date of the first drawing; and the interest rate on drawings charged to poorer borrowers could be subsidized, perhaps from a special account subscribed to by high-income members of the Fund, or out of the proceeds of further gold sales by the Fund.

The proposed new facility has a number of advantages: it represents a realistic response to the fact that many developing countries suffer from structural imbalances which need to be adjusted to more gradually than is permitted under traditional Fund procedures; it is technically feasible; and it could be brought into operation fairly quickly. There are, however, a number of disadvantages. Developed countries may not be persuaded of the need for such a facility, particularly now that repayments under the Extended Fund Facility can be made over a period up to 10 years, and now that the World Bank is beginning to move into the field of structural adjustment programmes. Some developing countries may be less in favour of a new facility made available through the Fund — which they see as dominated by developed countries — than of one made available through some new institution in which they have a more equitable share of the decision-making. Other aspects to be considered, in the context of a massive transfer of resources, are the revolving nature of the new facility, requiring repayments of principal to be completed within 10 years; and the question of whether such a facility, if established, would be likely on its own to be on a scale sufficient to make a significant contribution to the problem.

Private international banks

A large part of the recycling of the OPEC surpluses which took place after the first oil-price increase in 1973–4 was handled by the private banking system. Essentially, OPEC surpluses were deposited with the international banks, and on the basis of these deposits the banks made loans to developing, and some developed, countries. Although this mechanism will continue to operate to some degree, there are a number of reasons for doubting whether it can by itself make a satisfactory contribution to the need to transfer resources from North to South during the 1980s.

One reason for doubt lies in the concern that a number of international banks have begun to feel about their capital to asset ratios, given the enormous increase in their lending over the past decade. There are indications that some banks are becoming increasingly reluctant to accept further OPEC deposits, because of the erosion of their capital/assets ratios to which the on-lending of these deposits would lead.[2] (Some might suggest that there may also be greater reluctance on the part of some OPEC countries to deposit funds with the American-based international banks, in view of the US action in freezing Iranian bank deposits in November 1979.)

A second and more specific reason for counting less on this mechanism in the future lies in the high exposure of the international banks in precisely those mainly middle-income developing countries — Argentina, Brazil, Mexico, Korea, Taiwan and the Philippines — whose good creditworthiness made them the most attractive recipients of loans in the aftermath of the 1973–4 oil price increase. Conventional considerations of banking prudence, enhanced by the rise in these countries' debt-service ratios, are already making the banks reluctant to increase their lending to them; while there is no more incentive to the banks to take the risk of lending to less creditworthy countries than there was before.

Quite apart from considerations of risk, two other features of bank lending reduce its suitability as a vehicle for massive transfers of resources. One is that the maturity of bank loans is typically too short to answer the need of the South for capital on a long-term basis. The other, and more important, feature is that the commercial rates of interest charged by the international banks put such a source of finance on any substantial scale out of the reach of many of the poorer developing countries.

Thus the two main weaknesses of private bank lending as a vehicle for transferring resources from North to South lie essentially in the banks' fears of default on further loans, and the inability of many developing countries to service loan capital on the commercial terms charged by the banks. This suggests the importance of two particular mechanisms: interest-rate subsidies and guarantees.

Interest-rate subsidies would bridge the gap between the market rates charged by the private banks and the rates which developing countries can afford to pay. Thus in cases where it was deemed appropriate for resources to be transferred on IDA terms, a subsidy would be needed for virtually the whole of the market rate of interest. In other cases, where loans on the World Bank's 'Third Window' terms seemed suitable, only about half the market rate of interest would need to be subsidized.

Guarantees would provide an assurance to banks and other private sector institutions that funds lent to developing countries would be serviced and eventually redeemed. The basic rationale of a guarantee system is that by removing the risk of default on particular loans it can lead to an increase in the volume of private sector lending to the South; and the increase in the output and incomes of developed countries eventually generated by these extra resource flows far more than compensates for the cost of any guarantees which they may have to honour.[3]

The potential importance of interest-free subsidies and guarantees is attested by the frequency with which one or other mechanism features in the different proposals put forward during the last few years, the most important of which are briefly surveyed below.

Venezuelan proposal[4]

The aim would be to transfer something like $16–20 billion a year, for five or ten years, from OECD and OPEC countries to developing countries. The funds would be made available on a long-term basis, varying from 12 to 20 years. To some extent they would be targeted towards projects whose associated imports would tend to match OECD industries with spare capacity, or towards sectors where world supply bottlenecks threatened to appear in the medium term. Funds would be raised in two different ways. Of the total, something like 75 per cent would be raised by selling 'OPEC Development Bonds' in international capital markets; OPEC countries themselves would agree to purchase a quarter or so of these bonds, and would act as 'first guarantor' of the bonds taken up by private investors. The remaining 25 per cent of the money would be subscribed by developed countries, out of existing or increased aid allocations. In consequence, a quarter or so of the total fund could be channelled to basic needs projects in the least developed countries on concessional terms, the remainder would be lent at market rates, but at a 12–20 year maturity, to bankable projects in other developing countries. In both cases, funds would be disbursed through the World Bank family.

The main advantage of the Venezuelan proposal – apart from the fact that it is conceived on a scale more commensurable with the size of the problem than some other proposals – lies in the guarantee which the OPEC countries would provide to private investors. This might permit substantial new private funds to be tapped for on-lending to developing countries, though the long maturity envisaged for some of the bond issue (up to 20 years) might involve some increase in interest rates. If, however, the OPEC guarantee was not considered by potential investors to be sufficient, and it was necessary – a possibility envisaged by the proposal – to designate the World Bank as a 'second guarantor', the attraction of the proposal would be diminished, since the presumption would have to be that such guarantees could only be provided at the expense of guarantees or disbursements elsewhere in the World Bank's field of operations. The question thus arises of how far the proposal would in practice lead to an increased flow of non-concessional funds. Moreover, this question arises in even more acute form in the case of the quarter or so of the total disbursements which it would be intended to make on concessional terms. It is hard to see why the proposal should lead to any significant increase in the aid allocations of the developed countries; and so the result of the scheme being put into operation might be no more than to switch some aid funds from one channel to another.

Mexican proposal[5]

The Mexican proposal had as its main objective the marrying of excess capacity in the capital goods industries of developed countries with the unmet need for capital goods in developing countries. It was proposed to establish a fund of $15 billion, to be disbursed over a three- to five-year period in the form of loans with a maturity of 15 years or so. The fund would be financed by the issue of 15-year bonds on the international capital markets, and these bonds would be made attractive to private sector investors by being guaranteed by the governments of developed (and perhaps some developing) countries. The incentive to governments either to subscribe to the bond issue themselves or to guarantee the value of bonds taken up by private institutions would be that the loans made to finance projects or sector programmes in developing countries could only be used to purchase capital goods from other developing countries or from developed countries whose governments had subscribed to, or provided guarantees for, the bond issue. Thus the presumption is that the prospect of additional output and employment in their capital goods industries would persuade these governments to provide guarantees, particularly since loans would only be made for projects which the World Bank or other managing institution expected to yield an acceptable rate of return, thus rendering remote the likelihood of guarantees actually being called on.

The advantage of the proposal (as of the Venezuelan proposal, though this one is on a considerably smaller scale) is that by providing guarantees to private sector investors it might lead to the tapping of new financial resources in the North for transfer to the South. Moreover, developed country governments are given a specific incentive to act as guarantors; and the fact that it would be developed country rather than OPEC governments that would provide the guarantees, and the loans would be made available only to bankable projects, might enhance the attractiveness of the bond issue to the international capital markets, by comparison with the Venezuelan proposal. On the other hand, the scheme would mainly be of assistance to middle-income countries with the ability to absorb more funds at commercial rates, since (at any rate in the original proposal) no provision was made for interest subsidies to poorer countries; and although there is no reason why the scheme should not incorporate such subsidies, the question would arise of how they could be financed. Another area of doubt relates to the proposal's practicality: how far it is feasible, or even desirable, to restrict loans to purchases of particular categories of goods in particular countries; how problems of 'switching' could be dealt with, etc.

OECD/DAC proposal[6]

Like the Venezuelan and Mexican proposals, the essence of this scheme is to increase the flow of non-concessional private capital to developing countries by providing it with a form of guarantee. In this case the focus would be on the private international banks, which would be encouraged to expand their loans to developing countries by associating such loans with World Bank lending under an extended provision of 'co-financing'. The security of private funds lent to developing countries through this mechanism would be enhanced by the 'cross-default' provisions, which would stipulate that defaulting on the private element in the package would be deemed a default on the World Bank component as well, with the serious consequences for the defaulting country which that would entail. Loans would be made on commercial terms to projects in developing countries which promised an acceptable rate of return. There might be some emphasis on projects in such sectors as food and energy, where supply constraints potentially threaten the growth of both developed and developing countries, though such emphasis is not necessarily an essential part of the basic proposal.

One advantage of the scheme is that it would presumably have the backing of OECD countries. Another is that since it consists of an expansion of co-financing schemes which already exist on a modest scale, there should be no doubts about its technical feasibility. A third advantage is that experience suggests that bank funds which are lent as part of a co-financing arrangement are likely to have a somewhat greater maturity, and carry a slightly lower rate of interest, than would otherwise be the case.

The main drawback of the scheme might be seen as lying in precisely those features which would make it acceptable to the OECD countries: the extra flows envisaged seem to be fairly small in relation to the problem; and since they would be entirely on non-concessional terms, countries lacking commercially viable projects of the kind private lenders are likely to take an interest in would not benefit from the proposal except to the, probably limited, extent to which greater flows of non-concessional lending to middle-income countries led to some displacement of ODA in favour of the poorest countries.

Algerian–Venezuelan proposal[7]

All the mechanisms for increasing the transfer of resources from the North (and OPEC) to the South which have been discussed so far would work through either the IMF or the World Bank family (though the Mexican proposal refers briefly to the possibility of some new institution). The Algerian–Venezuelan proposal, on the other hand, specifically envisages a new institution — a Third World Development Agency, based on the OPEC Special Fund created in 1976 — which would recycle OPEC surpluses *directly* to the Third World.

The underlying rationale of the new Agency 'would be its ability to strengthen the solidarity of OPEC countries and other developing countries by *pooling their credit capacities* for the benefit of all developing countries'.[8] More specifically, it would 'provide funds for general development projects — particularly those projects likely to promote trade amongst developing countries and lessen their dependence on imported energy'. It seems clear that funds would be provided on both concessional and non-concessional terms — 'the conditions of financing should be *suited to the general economic situation of each country*, its degree of dependency on imported energy, and the situation of its balance of payments' (p. 12); and for the promotion of certain projects, 'specially adapted terms will be given to those countries which are worst affected or least developed' (p. 15).

It is proposed that the authorized capital of the Agency would be $20 billion, though this amount could be increased from time to time. Half of this capital would be paid in, and the other half would be callable.[9] On the basis of the implicit guarantees represented by this paid-in and callable capital, bonds would be issued in international capital markets at commercial rates of interest, though it is envisaged that initially a significant proportion of the bond issue would be taken up by the OPEC countries themselves.

The strength of the Algerian–Venezuelan proposal lies in

the fact that OPEC unquestionably has the resources to subscribe to the Agency on the scale contemplated; that such paid-in and callable capital subscriptions should act as a sufficient guarantee for additional private sector capital, possibly on a substantial scale, to be invested in the Agency's bonds; and that explicit provision is made for the subsidization of the interest rates charged to developing countries in appropriate cases. Detailed features of the mechanism, however, need to be worked out and agreed on: how the capital subscriptions are to be allocated between OPEC members, what proportion of the subscribed capital should be used for subsidies, what degree of subsidy should apply to which categories of projects and countries, etc. In principle, however, it seems clear that given an OPEC commitment to it, the proposed mechanism is eminently viable, and could promote a significant increase in the volume of resources transferred to non-oil developing countries. (Further aspects of the proposal are discussed in Section III.)

III   Institutions

The IMF

The difficulties involved in using the IMF as an instrument for massive transfers of resources to the developing countries are well known. Essentially, the Fund sees its job as lending money on a fairly short-term basis, and on precisely-defined conditions, to countries which have got into balance of payments difficulties and need some temporary assistance in order to get back on an even keel. The Fund does not regard itself as a development institution; nor do the developed countries which dominate its policies.

Nevertheless, in recent years the pressure of events has to some extent modified the Fund's philosophy and behaviour. Particularly since the huge current imbalances thrown up by the first round of oil-price increases in 1973–4, it has come to recognize that balance of payments deficits which are too large to be financed on acceptable terms by private capital inflows are not always the consequence of economic mismanagement, and cannot always be eliminated within a year or two. The Oil Facility established in 1974 was one piece of testimony to this shift in perception; the creation of the Extended Fund Facility, the recent extension of repayments under it from eight years to ten years, and the changes in the IMF's guidelines in 1979 were others.

Further modifications of Fund philosophy and practice can be envisaged. A Medium-term Facility of the kind discussed earlier could be established and, provided it operated under first credit tranche conditionality, could provide valuable resource transfers to developing countries in the medium term. Future allocations of Special Drawing Rights could be skewed in a way that favoured developing countries. The resources available to the Fund to back the expansion of existing facilities, or the creation of new ones, could be augmented by borrowing in world capital markets or direct from OPEC.

When all is said and done, however, the fact remains that the Fund is not, and is unlikely in the near future to become, a primary vehicle for the transfer of resources to developing countries on a scale, or at a maturity, or on conditions, commensurate with what is needed. That task must mainly be discharged by other new or existing insitutions.

The World Bank

Several of the proposed new mechanisms for transferring resources from North to South which were discussed earlier would involve the World Bank as administrator and dispenser of funds. This implies a presumption that the constraint on transfers of resources lies in the availability of funds rather than the Bank's capacity to use these funds effectively. This is certainly true as far as concessional funds are concerned, but it is not clear how true it is of funds which are to be made available at market rates. The World Bank has already taken steps to double the value of its capital, so as to support a much larger volume of non-concessional lending. Moreover, many observers consider that it could, without significant damage to its credit standing, increase the ratio of its loans to its authorized capital from the present very conservative 1:1 to 2:1 or even 3:1. This would result in a further big increase in its ability to provide non-concessional loans to developing countries.

The question arises, however, of how far and how fast the Bank could disburse substantially greater sums, whether raised by an increase in its capital or a change in its gearing ratio, or through the kind of mechanisms envisaged in some of the proposals discussed earlier. For the main role of the Bank has for many years now been seen as one of financing projects in developing countries which promise to yield an acceptable rate of return. During the past 25 years well over 90 per cent of the funds made available by the Bank have gone towards such projects. It is at least questionable whether the process of identifying, preparing and implementing such projects could be increased at anything like a fast enough rate to square with the size of the necessary transfer of resources from North to South as seen in a macroeconomic context (though the difficulties might be somewhat eased by providing more funds on a decentralized basis, for example through the Regional Development Banks.)

A possible way of dealing with this problem would be for the Bank to make a big move in the direction of providing programme, rather than project, assistance. To some extent, indeed, the new emphasis the Bank has been putting on structural adjustment lending over the past year or so can be regarded as a response of this kind. However, such a move, on any significant scale, could create further difficulties. Programme lending — which is precisely what the IMF does, though on a short time-scale — involves the application of some form of conditionality: otherwise the borrower is being given *carte blanche* to do what he likes with the money, and the lender can have no assurance that the borrower will be in a position to service or redeem the loan. Thus a dilemma arises. The Bank could get itself involved in the business of devising conditions and performance criteria for its programme loans in order to be sure that its money was being used wisely: but the logic of this leads in the direction of the kind of stringency traditionally associated with the IMF. Alternatively, the Bank could make programme loans available on the basis of fairly broad and loose conditions. But this, even if it did not lead to actual defaults, could seriously damage the Bank's own credibility as a borrower in world capital markets — a credibility which

ultimately rests on the fact that most Bank loans have traditionally been made to projects which yield an acceptable
rate of return. In a technical sense, of course, Bank creditworthiness rests on the paid-in and callable capital from its
subscribers; but if these subscribers were in fact called on to
reimburse the Bank's bondholders for the consequences of
defaults on the Bank's programme loans, it is hard to believe
that there would not be a change either in Bank policies or
in the willingness of the developed countries to continue to
underwrite its activities.

The same problems do not arise in the case of concessional
funds: the World Bank family should have no difficulty in
making effective use of much larger concessional flows. But
the problem of concessional assistance has never been primarily one of the mechanisms or institutions used to disburse
it; it is one of the willingness of OECD or OPEC countries
to provide it.

A Third World Development Agency

The way in which the Third World Development Agency proposed by the Algerians and Venezuelans might work was
discussed in the previous section. As a new institution,
backed by OPEC money, it should be able to generate a
substantial increase in the flow of resources to non-oil
developing countries. The hope of its sponsors that the new
body would strengthen the solidarity of Third World countries might well be realized, since from the start it would be
set up, financed and operated by Third World countries
themselves — unlike the IMF and World Bank, which were
set up by, and are still dominated by, a handful of developed
countries. At the same time, it would be a mistake to exag-
gerate the say which borrowers, rather than lenders, are likely
to have in the lending policies and conditions of the proposed
Agency, even if both groups do belong to the Third World.

A number of problems would arise in setting up and
operating the new Agency. Some of these — such as the need
to recruit or train staff qualified in project appraisal, etc. —
would merely be a matter of time. Others raise more fundamental issues, similar in some cases to those discussed earlier
in connection with an expansion of lending by the World

Bank. How far, for example, would the Agency concentrate its lending on identifiable projects which promised a satisfactory rate of return, and how far on satisfying the more general needs of non-oil developing countries, such as support for measures reinforcing regional integration, expenditure on broad measures of social development, or the financing of balance of payments deficits? The greater the emphasis on project lending, the greater would be the need to avoid competing with the World Bank for viable projects whose total number may prove difficult to expand at the rate necessary to absorb the sums available. If, on the other hand, the main emphasis is to be on long-term programme lending, the same question arises as in the case of a major expansion of programme lending by the World Bank: what conditions are to be applied, and what performance indicators are to be monitored? Tight conditions will reduce the ability of many developing countries to benefit from the activities of the new Agency. Loose conditions, on the other hand, may damage the credibility of the Agency's bonds, and significantly reduce the amounts of capital it can raise.

This dilemma should not prove insoluble, and should be easier to solve the greater is the amount of concessional funds, to be used to finance interest rate subsidies or in other ways, that OPEC countries are willing to make available to the new Agency. Thus the effectiveness of the new Agency is likely to depend in no small part on the generosity of its OPEC subscribers.

A World Development Fund

The Brandt Commission pinpointed the case for a new institution: 'What is needed essentially is a bridge between the long-term project financing available from such institutions as the World Bank and the short-term adjustment finance available from the IMF.'[10] The solution it proposed was an institution that might be called a World Development Fund. It would have universal membership, and would thus offer an opportunity for developed and developing countries to cooperate on a basis of more equal partnership. The main thrust of the new organization would be in the direction of programme lending, including support for measures to increase trade among developing countries, to undertake exploration for minerals, etc. So far from competing with the World Bank and the IMF, it would 'complement and complete the existing structure'.[11] Its long-term programme lending would help the disbursement of World Bank projects held up by the shortage of domestic resources, and could also help to keep countries from reaching the kind of crisis situation in which they have to go to the IMF for balance of payments adjustment finance. Many of the new Fund's operations could go through co-financing arrangements with the World Bank and the Regional Development Banks; and the bulk of its lending would go through regional and sub-regional institutions.

The crucial point about the World Development Fund, as envisaged by the Brandt Commission, is that the great bulk of its resources would come from government contributions, and not from private institutions seeking a market rate of return on their investment. Sources of these contributions would be the rapid achievement of the 0.7 per cent target for ODA by all those countries committed to it, and an increase in the target to 1 per cent of GNP by the year 2000; and, more generally, by the introduction of 'automatic mechanisms' which would yield revenue from a wide range of countries on a basis which took progressive account of their wealth: a levy on international trade, with built-in adjustments to ensure that its incidence was equitable in relation to different countries' GNP, would be one possible way of putting this idea into practice.

With this method of financing the World Development Fund, the predominance in its operations of long-term programme lending makes perfectly good sense. It would be relieved of the need — imposed on the World Bank by the requirements of the private investors who provide the bulk of its funds — to concentrate on projects which yielded a commercially acceptable rate of return. It would also be relieved of the need — imposed on the IMF by the traditionally short time-horizon within which it operates — to provide programme assistance only on strict conditions which promise a speedy return to balance of payments equilibrium. It should, in fact, be able to fill the role allotted it — that of bridging the gap between long-term Bank project financing and short-term IMF programme financing.

But the obverse of this is clear: the success of a World Development Fund would depend on the willingness of Northern and OPEC countries to provide official development assistance, in one form or another, on a much larger scale than at present. Without such willingness, the WDF would be stillborn. In this event, one would be forced to accept that a massive transfer of resources from North to South would depend not on satisfying governments and peoples in the North that effective steps were being taken to alleviate world poverty, but on satisfying private investors in the North that their money was being lent on terms that promised a secure and commercially acceptable rate of return. This latter is obviously a much more stringent requirement, probably leading to less transfer of resources, and certainly to less alleviation of poverty.

IV   Concluding observations

Most of the mechanisms which have been proposed for an increased transfer of resources from North to South rely heavily on the possibility of mobilizing more private capital. The presumption is that there are plenty of investment opportunities in the South that would yield a market rate of return, and that it should be possible to channel some of the huge funds now invested in, say, the Euromarkets in this direction. Nevertheless, lending to developing countries can look a risky business to private banks and other private institutions – particularly now that huge private loans have already been made to those countries which seem in principle most creditworthy, with a correspondingly dramatic effect on their debt service ratios.

The obvious solution to this problem is to provide such investors with some form of guarantee, to ensure that the mutual benefits that can accrue to developing countries and Northern investors should not be frustrated by the fears of these investors that one loan on which there is a default should be the one to which they have subscribed. However, in the last resort such guarantees can only be provided to

Northern private investors by Northern governments. And if there is a prospect that such guarantees may have to be honoured (even if they never do in practice have to be honoured) there is a danger that they will be given only at the cost of a reduction in guarantees, or even in aid allocations, somewhere else in the system. Therefore the question of how far mechanisms which involve the provision of guarantees will in fact lead to significant additions to the transfer of resources is a very real one; and though the presumption is that they will, it is impossible to be dogmatic.

A similar question arises in relation to the interest subsidies which will be needed if poorer countries or sectors are to derive any benefit from increased transfers of private capital. If these subsidies are financed out of aid allocations, or IMF gold sales, or subscriptions by developed countries *which would not otherwise have taken place* then one can be assured that *additional* concessional flows have become available. But it may be difficult to know whether or not such allocations would otherwise have taken place; and if the presumption is that aid budgets, IMF gold sales, etc., are determined by factors other than the simple availability of mechanisms for disbursing the money, the conclusion is likely to be a negative one.

The problems encountered with mechanisms designed to channel private funds to developing countries would be partially avoided in the case of the proposed Third World Development Agency, because of the sizeable element of OPEC capital subscriptions which might be involved; and very largely avoided in the case of the World Development Fund, which would rely for its financing on aid allocations in one form or another. But the avoidance of one set of problems can only be achieved by finding a solution to another: the reluctance of governments and peoples in the North to pay higher taxes to help governments and peoples in the South.

A rational and praiseworthy attempt to provide a solution to this problem takes the form of stressing the mutual interests of North and South. In particular it is argued that financial transfers to the South will lead to more investment, rising incomes and rising imports in the South, which will in turn lead to a rise in output and investment, and a fall in unemployment, in the North. But such an argument may overlook the belief currently held by many Northern governments that there will be no revival of investment or growth in the North until inflation is brought under control, and that until this happens there can be no relaxation of the North's deflationary economic policies. Such a belief may appear absurd to the South, and to many in the North as well; but it is a belief which cannot, in the present climate, be ignored.

Notes

1 Proposal put forward in UNDP/UNCTAD Project INT/75/015, *The Balance of Payments Adjustment Process in Developing Countries: Report to the Group of Twenty-four*, 2 January 1979, para. 35 (vii).

2 Lal Jayawardena, 'The Massive Transfer of Resources to Developing Countries', Chapter 3 of this book.

3 For a brief account of some different types of guarantee arrangement see Appendix 1 of *The World Economic Crisis: a Commonwealth Perspective*, Commonwealth Secretariat, 1980.

4 This proposal was outlined by President Perez at a press conference after the December 1977 meeting of OPEC Ministers at Caracas. It should not be confused with the proposal submitted by Algeria and Venezuela to the December 1979 OPEC ministerial meeting at Caracas, which is discussed later in the chapter.

5 Proposal put forward by the Mexican government at the meeting of the Development Committee in Mexico City, April 1978.

6 OECD, *A Proposal for Stepped-Up Co-Financing for Investment in Developing Countries*, Paris, May 1979.

7 *Joint Proposal by the Algerian and Venezuelan Delegations on the Need for Additional Financial Cooperation between OPEC Member Countries and Other Developing Countries*, submitted by Algeria and Venezuela to the meeting of OPEC ministers held at Caracas in December 1979.

8 Abdelkader Sid Ahmed, Ministry of Energy and Petrochemical Industries, Algiers, 'The role of the new OPEC Development Agency', Chapter 2 of this book.

9 The Agency might start operations at the beginning of 1981 with paid-in capital of $5 billion out of an initial total of $10 billion; the overall total of $20 billion would be reached by 1983.

10 *Brandt Commission Report*, Pan edition, p. 234, 1981.
11 Ibid., p. 253.

7 THE WHY AND HOW OF FUNDING LDC DEBT

John Williamson*

This chapter was prepared as part of a study entitled 'Framework for International Financial Cooperation' sponsored by the Centre for Research on the New International Economic Order, Oxford. It was subsequently presented to the Second International Conference on Latin American and Caribbean Financial Developments at Caraballeda, Venezuela, in April 1981. The chapter develops an idea first sketched in Williamson (1977) and subsequently elaborated in the course of a short visit to the Council on Foreign Relations, New York. The author is indebted to participants in a number of seminars where the topic was discussed in the course of that visit, as well as the discussants at Oxford and Caraballeda, for many helpful comments that have influenced both the form of and the argumentation for the proposal presented in the chapter.

It is the thesis of this chapter that there exists a rather general international interest, embracing borrowers, lenders and third parties, in achieving a marked lengthening in the maturity structure of the debt of developing countries. Section 1 explains the reasons for this belief. Section 2 develops a set of proposals for an international initiative intended to facilitate general, large-scale, long-term borrowing by developing countries. Many details of the scheme could, no doubt, be varied, but the proposals are intended to complement each other to form a coherent package.

1. Why

I take it as axiomatic that a substantial level of borrowing by developing countries is normal, rational and desirable.

* Pontifícia Universidade Católica do Rio de Janeiro, Brazilia.

Real returns can be expected to be higher in capital-short developing countries than in either capital-rich developed countries or oil-rich, high-savings countries; it is therefore appropriate to expect the international financial system to facilitate a flow of real resources from the latter to the former. The need for capital inflows to a developing country can be expected to vary over time, not just for obvious cyclical reasons, but also on a secular basis and in response to shocks. The typical secular pattern is of an initial rise as development gets under way and absorptive capacity runs ahead of the ability to generate savings domestically, followed by a decline and ultimately a reversal as savings rise in response to the increase in income. Shocks, such as the oil price increase, can produce an economic case for above normal borrowing for substantial periods while long-run programmes involving structural adaptation are implemented.

Although a good deal of alarm has been expressed about debt burdens in recent years, some of the conventional measures suggest that the 'burden of the debt' has increased surprisingly little over the 1970s, and indeed remains reasonable or even modest by historical standards. The conventional measures relate either the stock of (external) debt, or the annual flow of debt-service payments, to either GNP/GDP or 'exports', for which the conceptually-appropriate measure is clearly total receipts on current account. Arthur Lewis (1977) quotes a figure of 1.8 for the ratio of total external debt to exports of all developing countries in 1972, which he contrasts with ratios in 1913 of about 2.25 for low-debt capital-importing countries (China, India and Japan), 4.8 for Australia, 5.2 for Latin America and 8.6 for Canada. Data based on the World Bank's Debtor Reporting System show only a modest increase in the ratio of 'public and publicly-guaranteed long-term external debt' to exports of goods and services for all non-oil developing countries, from some 70 per cent in 1973 to 86 per cent in 1978, with a probable decline to around 80 per cent in 1979. (The bulk of the difference between these figures for 1973 and Arthur Lewis's figures for 1972 is accounted for by his inclusion of private debt — some 38 per cent of his total — in the numerator, and the inclusion of exports of services in the denominator of the alternative figures.) The analogous debt/GDP ratio rises from under 14 per cent in 1973 to around 19 per cent in 1978–9. Similarly, Arthur Lewis cites a figure of average debt-service payments to exports for all developing countries of 23 per cent in 1972, as against some 60 per cent for Argentina in 1890, while Volcker (1980) shows a ratio (based only on public and publicly-guaranteed debt) rising from some 9 per cent in 1973 to 17.5 per cent in 1978 for non-oil LDCs. Despite the difficulties of making exact comparisons, these figures give little ground for alarmism about the current debt situation of developing countries in general.

Nevertheless, such aggregate figures may conceal important variations between countries. It is convenient to quote the statistics of one heavily-indebted country, namely Brazil, that happen to be readily available. The ratios quoted in Brazil are 'net (of reserves) (total) debt to exports (of goods)', which has risen from about unity in 1973 to some 2.6 in 1979, and 'debt service to exports', which rose from 41 per cent in 1973 to 68 per cent in 1979. By comparison with Arthur Lewis's figures for the previous great age of international lending (before the First World War), it seems that Brazilian external debt is not abnormally high at present, but that there is no basis for an equally sanguine conclusion regarding debt-service payments.

The reason that debt-service payments are historically high while debt is not lies in high inflation and the short maturities of most current debt. Although the maturity of Brazilian borrowing lengthened again in the late 1970s, in comparison with the drastic shortening initially prompted by the oil price increase, the typical loan currently taken by Brazil is something like a nine-year Euro-credit. This compares with bonds of 20 or 30 years that were the rule before the First World War. Moreover, the Euro-credit has a floating interest rate set perhaps one or two per cent above LIBOR, which in the past year exceeded 20 per cent and stayed over 15 per cent for months on end, in comparison with the interest rates of perhaps 4 or 5 per cent that were the norm before 1914.

Table 7.1 shows the sensitivity of debt-service payments to

Table 7.1

Nominal interest rate (%)	3			9			15		
Maturity (years)	5	10	50	5	10	50	5	10	50
Nominal interest payments	3	3	3	9	9	9	15	15	15
Nominal amortization	20	10	2	20	10	2	20	10	2
Debt-service payments	23	13	5	29	19	11	35	25	17
Debt-service/exports* (%)	46	26	10	58	38	26	70	50	34
Real amortization	20	10	2	26	16	8	32	22	14

* The debt:export ratio is assumed to be 2.

both inflation, which is completely reflected in the interest rate, and maturity. Debt is assumed to be 100, and amortization to be spread out evenly. A rise in inflation from zero to 12 per cent raises nominal interest payments from 3 to 15, while a reduction in maturity from 50 years to 5 raises amortization payments from 2 to 20. Combined, the two factors can make a seven-fold difference to the debt-service: exports ratio. Short maturities and high nominal interest rates can convert a historically-modest level of indebtedness into a historically very high call on export earnings.

It is, of course, perfectly true that these heavy debt-service payments do not represent a charge on the country's net worth. Both high amortization and that part of the nominal interest rate that simply compensates for inflation result in a reduction in the country's real foreign indebtedness. For this reason, the two factors have been combined in a measure called 'real amortization' in the final row of the table. Naturally, since the real interest rate is the same throughout the table, a high debt-service:exports ratio is inevitably associated with high real amortization, and therefore with the possibility of contracting additional foreign loans without increasing the conventional measures of the burden of the debt. Debt can be rolled over.

The critical question is therefore whether the need to roll over debt repeatedly, which is a consequence of high real amortization, does or does not impose real economic costs on a borrower. It is instructive to consider this question by a simple formalization of the policy problem confronting the authorities of a small open capital-importing economy; it simplifies matters greatly if we can assume the terms of trade to be constant as well as exogenous. Let W = intertemporal welfare, U = instantaneous social utility, C = consumption, δ = the social discount rate, K = capital stock, Y = output, D = real gross foreign debt, B = the flow of new borrowing, A = real amortization of foreign debt (so $D = B - A$), R = reserves, r_1 = real rate of interest paid on foreign debt, and r_2 = real rate of interest received on reserves. Then a standard neo-classical formulation of the problem facing the authorities is that of seeking to maximize

$$W = \int_0^\infty U(C)e^{-\delta t}dt \qquad U_1 > 0, U_{11} < 0$$

subject to the constraints (a) that reserves never be negative, $R \geqslant 0$, and (b) that absorption be no greater than full employment output plus foreign borrowing minus net debt-service payments minus reserve accumulation, or

$$C + \dot{K} \leqslant Y(K, \ldots) + B - A - r_1 D + r_2 R - \dot{R}.$$

Why should high real amortization payments A threaten W, given that their impact on the balance of payments, and hence on real resources, can be compensated by increasing borrowing B without increasing debt D? It is immediately clear from the structure of the problem that there exist circumstances in which the level of A has no effect on W. This would be the case if B were always constrained only by price, and the relevant interest rate r_1 were a function only of D. Note that in these circumstances it will always pay to maintain $R = 0$ (assuming $r_1 > r_2$). That is, in such circumstances the ability to borrow provides infinite liquidity, and hence there is no point in buying liquidity by holding reserves – or by contracting long-term debt.

Conversely, the absence of the special circumstances delineated above creates the possibility of gains from holding liquid assets – and, analogously, of limiting the extent to which one is subject to an obligation to repay at short notice. If borrowing increases in cost, or if the possibilities tend to vanish entirely, at certain times, then liquidity fulfils the function of enabling a country to avoid compressing absorption $(C + K)$ unduly at those times. The obvious way of formalizing this in the above model would be to assume $Y(\ )$ to be a stochastic variable; a negative supply shock would then force a cut in absorption unless it were possible to draw down reserves or to borrow more. The possibility of borrowing more will be unattractive or even unavailable, to the extent that borrowing possibilities tend to deteriorate at times when the balance of payments is under pressure. The larger is amortization, the larger will be the level of borrowing that must be undertaken on such unfavourable terms in order to maintain a given level of absorption — and hence the worse those terms must be expected to be.

Thus the crucial factor in evaluating whether a high level of amortization imposes real costs is that of whether credit-worthiness as perceived by lenders, and thus borrowing possibilities, vary with the short-/medium-run state of the economy, and in particular with its balance of payments position. Is there any truth in the old adage that a banker is always willing to lend to anyone who does not really need the money? Or can we join those who reassure us that debt can always be rolled over because bankers realize that such rolling over is necessary to safeguard their assets?

Given that any one bank owns no more than a small fraction of a country's external debt, it is always possible for an individual bank to reduce (or even eliminate) its exposure to a country that it has come to believe to be a bad risk, provided that it moves before most other banks do. This creates a free rider problem with a vengeance (since you pay unless you are among the first off the bus), which explains the historically frequent occurrence of financial panics. Of course, past panics have often been preceded by reassurances that panics are a thing of the past because people have learnt there is no such thing as a free ride, but the reassurances proved misplaced because the premise was false. Some people *can* have a free ride and it is only realistic to recognize that they will sometimes try to take one.

A borrowing country's vulnerability to a bankers' attempt to 'get off the bus' certainly depends on the level of real amortization payments that it is committed to making.

Hence it follows that the amount that bankers can prudently lend *ex ante* (before they know whether they would manage to get off the bus in the event of a crisis developing) depends inversely on A — despite the fact that each of them will quite rationally try to insist on arrangements regarding his own loans that involve high amortization. And that is surely why there is today nervousness about Brazil's foreign debt, despite the facts that Brazil has historically behaved as a conscientious debtor and that her debt is currently modest, relative to exports and certainly relative to GNP, compared with the levels that were commonplace prior to the First World War. What is undermining her creditworthiness and limiting her borrowing possibilities, is that her debt-service ratio is already high by historical standards and is still rising.

The conclusion I draw is therefore that there would be real gains, in terms of reducing the vulnerability of borrowing countries and of increasing the borrowing that they could prudently undertake, from achieving a major funding of LDC debt and thus reducing the time stream of real amortization payments associated with a given level of real indebtedness. This potential gain arises from a classic cause of market failure, namely the free rider problem generated by the fact that lenders have an incentive to act individually in a way that is prone to convert an adverse turn of events into a panic for a heavily-indebted country.

2. How

In designing a mechanism to permit long-term borrowing by developing countries, and thus secure a funding of their debt, it is natural to start by asking why there is so little long-term borrowing at the present time. There is no doubt that a major part of the answer lies in inflation. As is well known, any certain future rate of inflation can be compensated for by an appropriate change in the nominal interest rate; the problem is that any fixed nominal rate of interest may lead either to heavy losses by the lenders (if inflation accelerates) or to a crippling debt burden on the borrowers (if it decelerates). It is the *variability* rather than the *level* of inflation that makes it impossible to establish fixed nominal interest rates on long-term bonds consistent with prudent risk aversion by both borrowers and lenders; but there is considerable evidence that rapid inflation does also tend to be variable inflation (for example, Jaffee and Kleiman, 1977). That is why medium-term lending has in recent years been conducted overwhelmingly with floating interest rates, which can and do vary in order to provide rough compensation for variations in inflation.

Reference to Table 7.1 will make it clear that floating interest rates do not provide a technique that would permit a major reduction in the burden of real amortization payments. With high rates of inflation, debt-service payments come to be dominated by interest payments once maturities reach the range already existing in Brazil, so that further stretching of those maturities could play only a modest (though still useful) role in reducing real amortization.

What is needed is a financial technique that will insulate the real value of debts, and also the effective maturity of debt, from unexpected variations in the rate of inflation. That can be accomplished by indexing debt, and in no other way. Accordingly, the basis of the proposal to be developed involves the issuance of indexed long-term bonds.

Mention of indexation seems to prompt hostile reflexes from two very different quarters. On the one hand, there are those with interests of LDC borrowers at heart who see this as liable to make more onerous the terms on which those countries can borrow. Real interest rates on LDC borrowing in the 1970s, they assert correctly, have been small or even zero; this would surely not be the case if borrowing were undertaken through an indexed bond, since a zero real interest rate would occur only if lenders decided deliberately that they would be content with a zero return. To that one can reply (a) that it is by no means clear that real interest rates will remain so low now that inflationary expectations have caught up with reality; (b) that if they do remain low, the borrowers may be faced with the even more unpleasant prospect of the world's major net creditors deciding to invest more by keeping their oil in the ground instead of buying so many financial assets; (c) that a higher real interest rate would within limits be a price worth paying in order to reduce the vulnerability created by short-term borrowing and to increase the total sums that could prudently be borrowed; and (d) that it seems that borrowers do in fact attach quite a high value to the latter point. (Brazil seems to have been content to pay 7–9 per cent on 10-year DM-denominated bonds in recent years, which looks like a positive enough real rate to me.)

On the other hand, there are those concerned with world macro-economic stability who regard any form of indexation as playing with fire. I am certainly not among those who dismiss fears of indexation out of hand: no one who has lived in Brazil recently is likely to doubt that widespread indexation of factor incomes can lead to a terrifyingly rapid translation of negative supply shocks into accelerating inflation, while those who have lived in Britain in the 1970s are also likely to fear the capacity of wage indexation to reinforce income claims that are collectively inconsistent with a satisfactory macro-economic equilibrium. There is also a persuasive case against the indexation of liquid assets, since this eliminates real balance effects, which are normally stabilizing. But to carry these legitimate objections over to the indexation of long-term debt is wrong: that case needs analysing on its own merits, which happen to be very different to either widespread indexation of factor incomes or that of liquid assets. Indexation of long-term debt would eliminate the redistribution of wealth that unexpectedly rapid inflation brings in an unindexed system, which is from creditor units to debtor units; to the extent that there is an expectation that the former will have a higher propensity to save than the latter, this effect will tend to be stabilizing. But far more important than this traditional type of effect would be any success that the scheme might enjoy in promoting funding. Long-term debt is less inflationary than short-term debt. This is not because, as sometimes seems to be implied, there is any reason to suppose that with unchanged net worth people will spend less if they hold long-term rather than short-term assets. Rather, the critical point is that the prices of illiquid long-term assets, and thus net worth, vary contra-cyclically, tending to fall in time of boom when everyone else is trying to spend, and to rise in recession when spending is weak. This provides an incentive to shift the *timing* of expenditures in a macro-economically-stabilizing manner. Because of this, a system with a large volume of long-term debt can expect over the years to have both less inflation and less unemployment than a system where debt is predominantly short term. With long-term and thus variable-priced debt, a substantial part of the financial adjustment needed to restore equilibrium in real markets following an exogenous demand shock can take the form of a revaluation in the price of debt. With liquid and thus fixed-price debt, in contrast, restoration of equilibrium requires that the necessary change in the real value of debt be effected either by a change in the price level or by a change in the quantity of debt. There is an obvious temptation to allow expansionary demand shocks to be cured by inflation, and contractionary shocks to be cured by the increased short-term debt created by a budget deficit, which in turn sets the stage for the next upturn in demand to lead to more inflation. A funding that substituted substantial variations in the price of real debt for this pernicious mechanism would bring benefits that extended beyond the borrowers and lenders to whom this proposal is addressed.

I conclude that the common objections to indexation are in this instance unpersuasive or downright wrong. They provide no good reason for eschewing indexation if it would permit the developing countries to borrow at long term. I therefore proceed to discuss the six principal questions that would need to be decided in order to permit the developing countries to borrow through the issue of indexed long-term bonds.

(a) Institutional sponsorship

It would be possible, and might indeed be worthwhile, to see whether indexation could enable individual countries to float their own long-term bonds. However, the scheme to be developed here involves the issuance of bonds by an international financial institution, which would effectively act as an agent for a collective of developing countries. This seems to offer two important advantages. First, it would permit the emergence of a relatively large market in a homogeneous bond, which can be expected to promote the marketability of the bond. Secondly, it would permit risk spreading by both borrowers and lenders. For example, it would be possible to vary borrowers' debt-service obligations with their ability to pay, as outlined in (f) below. Even more important, it would spread the lenders' risks over a number of borrowing countries. This would be particularly beneficial to the less advanced of the developing countries, who cannot in general borrow on their own credit at present.

There is reason to believe that this risk-spreading feature may be vital to win the interest of lenders, even without considering the special problem of the least-developed borrowers. This is suggested by the fact that certain borrowers with whom the market associates very low political risks, such as Canada and the World Bank, have been able to continue borrowing on long maturities of 20 or 30 years even during the inflationary 1970s. One can argue that the market has been irrational in being willing to lend to, say, Brazil on a maturity of 10 but not of 20 years, inasmuch as it is clear that lenders as a group will be in no position to liquidate their credits to Brazil in less than 20 years: the majority will have to roll over in one way or another. Nevertheless, it does seem to be a fact that lenders are reluctant to commit themselves to making long-term loans except when they judge the political risks to be negligible. This suggests that any scheme will be dependent on the ability to convince lenders that the risks are minimal. That in turn suggests that a collective of LDCs would be better placed to command market confidence than an individual country, while a collective of developing countries articulated through an international financial institution with a wider participation than that of borrowers alone should be even better placed to win market acceptance.

Given the desirability of having the scheme sponsored by an international financial institution, it would be necessary to decide which institution should act as sponsor. One possibility would be to create a new institution for this purpose. Personally I tend to react against proposals to create or reorganize institutions, since these usually represent mental escapism; they are the refuge of those unable to decide what needs to be done, who therefore propose charging a bureaucracy with the task of thinking on their behalf, which is normally a failure because bureaucracies are not very good at thinking up novel ideas, as opposed to thinking of reasons why novel ideas will not work and why any change at all needs lots more bureaucrats before it can be contemplated. Since any institutional reorganization seems to create such opportunities for bureaucratic aggrandizement (even when the initial intention is the reverse), a good general principle is to minimize institutional change. In the present context that points to the desirability of adapting an existing institution rather than founding a new one. Both the World Bank and the IMF command a reasonable measure of market respect, which would be invaluable in launching a scheme like this. Both dispose of assets (the Bank's accumulated profits, and the Fund's stock of redundant gold) that could be pledged with a view to providing assurance to potential lenders. Both already possess the type of staff and statistical services that operation of the scheme would require. As between the two, I venture no judgement: the danger is not, I suspect, that the two will fight for the privilege of enhancing their role in the world, but that both will prove too arthritic to conceive of the necessary reorientation of their operations, in which case it would be necessary to create a new institution after all. Given that this question has to remain open, I shall simply refer to the 'Sponsor' in the remainder of this chapter.

(b) Maturity

Borrowing by developing countries is fundamentally undertaken with the object of investing in the process of development, not in a particular project. Even in the most miraculous of cases, development is likely to continue to require over half a century to transform a country to the point where it is reasonable to start calling on it to make a net return transfer of real resources. Most loans made for shorter periods have to be rolled over, and therefore create the dangers previously discussed that are posed by high amortization payments. What is needed is a bond with a maturity long enough to avoid these frivolous amortization payments.

Fifty years is a nice round number that lies in the right ball-park.

I therefore assume that the Sponsor would periodically make an issue of 50-year bonds. Details of the issue process are discussed in (e) below.

(c) Indexation formula

As already argued, such long-term bonds would need to be indexed if they were to be attractive to both borrowers and lenders. This would imply a need for both a 'currency of account' in which the financial rights and obligations of the borrowers, the lenders and the Sponsor would be calculated, and a price index with which to revalue the sums specified in the currency of account. The SDR, now that it is defined in terms of a basket of currencies, provides the natural unit to adopt for the role of currency of account. Each borrower or lender dealing with the Sponsor would then specify the currency in which it wished to receive or make payments, which would then be made at the representative rate against the SDR for the day on which the transaction was due.

A bond would specify how many issue-date SDRs the Sponsor would pay the holder each year, as well as how many issue-date SDRs would be due the holder in 50 years' time in order to extinguish his claim on the Sponsor. It might be convenient to pay an annual interest coupon of SDR 30, and a final redemption of SDR 1,000 (both expressed in issue-date SDRs), so as to facilitate judgements about whether bond prices were high or low; if the historical norm of a 3 per cent real interest rate reasserted itself, the issue price and the subsequent market price would vary around SDR 1,000 (again in issue-date SDRs). The indexation formula would link the issue-date SDR with the current value of the SDR. If 'world prices' rose by 20 per cent, say, then the interest coupon payable on each bond would rise to SDR 36 (in current SDRs). Obviously the problem is to find a suitable index of 'world prices' for this purpose.

One possibility would be to use a price index of traded goods. An attraction of this solution is that it should be feasible to construct a universal index, rather than one based on the statistics of a limited number of countries. Another advantage is that this would most directly stabilize the purchasing power of investment income derived from holding the bond for a country with a typical import composition. As against those two considerations, one has to weigh the fact that the prices of traded goods — especially those of primary product — tend to be volatile. That would mean that the interest yield and ultimately the principal to be repaid would fluctuate in comparison with competing securities not just because of secular inflation, but also because of what are essentially changes in relative prices. While this might be tolerable where interest payments were concerned, it would surely introduce an unacceptably large random element into the determination of the principal to be repaid.

The alternatives are to use a weighted average of either consumer price indices (CPIs) or wholesale price indices (WPIs) in a number of leading countries. In either event, there is rather a natural way to choose the countries whose price indices are to be used and the weights to be attached to them: namely, to use the same countries and weights as those used to construct the SDR basket. This would directly stabilize the purchasing power of investment income over the relevant basket of goods bought from those countries, which collectively provide a large share of world exports. To the extent that purchasing power parity holds, the stabilization would be achieved even over a world-wide basket of goods.

There would seem to be two main differences between CPIs and WPIs that would be relevant to choosing which to adopt as the basis for indexation. One is that CPIs tend to rise faster because of the large weight they give to services, where productivity growth is slow. The share of services in international trade is smaller than that in the CPI but larger than that in the WPI, so that from the standpoint of stabilizing the trend purchasing power of the bond's payments over traded goods and services there may not be much to choose between the two. The other main difference is that changes in the WPI lead those in the CPI by several months. This would seem to give a marginal advantage to use of the WPI.

(d)   Guarantees versus Insurance

Although the bonds would be issued by the Sponsor, it would be impossible for the sponsoring institution to give a total guarantee without severely constraining the size of the operation. For example, bonds adequate to finance a half of the present LDC current-account deficit would exhaust the World Bank's total capital in little over two years – even if half that capital were not already pledged on outstanding loans, and even if the other half were not needed to sustain the existing plans of the Bank. It is simply not worth contemplating an operation the size of which would be constrained by the willingness of the developed countries to give guarantees – even if the provision of such guarantees would not raise the question of whether the borrowing guaranteed was additional to resources that would otherwise have been provided through some other channel. The basic concept must be that of the Sponsor acting on behalf of a collective of developing countries. The bonds issued by the Sponsor will therefore have to be, in the last resort, the liabilities of the countries on whose behalf the funds are being raised.

The countries that can be expected to account for the bulk of the funds raised are already judged creditworthy for substantial sums by the private market. The pooling of risks involved in issuance of bonds by the Sponsor can be expected to further increase the maturity and expand the sums that the market would be prepared to finance, even without guarantees from the Sponsor or third parties. But there could still be an important role for such guarantees, even though limited to sums far less than the total value of the bonds issued by the Sponsor. Without any guarantees, it is conceivable that the low creditworthiness of some countries might raise the cost of borrowing through the scheme to the point where some of the most creditworthy potential participants would decide that they could fare better independently. Their withdrawal would raise the cost of borrowing to the remaining members, provoke more withdrawals, and so on, in a vicious circle reminiscent of George Akerlof's (1970) 'market for lemons'. Given that there exist real benefits to be reaped through risk spreading, one can expect a limited sum of money used to provide guarantees to go a long way in promoting an LDC ability to borrow at long term.

Existing resources of the World Bank (in the form of its capital surplus) or the IMF (in the form of its remaining gold stocks) might provide the nucleus of a Guarantee Fund. Additional resources might be sought from at least two sources. The obvious one is the usual list of potential donors in the OECD and OPEC aid-giving countries. A less obvious source also seems worth exploring. Recall that the major burden of debt service under this scheme would commence only after the year 2030, by which time many of the countries that could be expected to make major use of the scheme in the next decade or two should have graduated to the point at which they will not only be able to afford some outward transfer of real resources, but at which they could and should be expected to become aid donors themselves. The international community has not yet established any explicit guidelines as to how this graduation process should be handled, but the implicit principle seems to be that once a country achieves a certain level of per capita income, it becomes liable to a moral obligation to devote at least 0.7 per cent of its GNP to overseas development assistance.[1] That would involve a rather abrupt transition. One way of modifying that abruptness would be to allow countries, for a limited period following their 'graduation', to satisfy their ODA obligations to a defined extent (which might even be tapered over time) by donating their own interest-bearing obligations to the Guarantee Fund. That would create no immediate charge on their balance of payments or real resources, although it would involve a genuine call on their net worth and contribution to the cause of development. Graduating countries would thus have the opportunity of assuming their new responsibilities promptly and earning the international respect that honouring the aid targets brings without the strains that could occur in a rapid untempered transition. Such provisions could create an expectation that the Guarantee Fund would grow to a substantial size before there arose any significant likelihood of its being called on. If the Fund grew embarrassingly large, the excess could no doubt be diverted into highly-concessional loans on the model established by the IMF's Trust Fund.

The administrative arrangements might therefore involve a separate Account for each issue of bonds, each of which would have a contingent claim on the Guarantee Fund. Each Account would acquire a series of claims on the countries that exercised their right to participate in that particular bond issue. Only if it suffered a default by one of those debtors would the Account exercise its claim on the Guarantee Fund. (Note that since other debtors to the Account would not be called on to make good the Account's losses, there would be no pressure for an isolated default to escalate.) The Account's creditors would suffer loss only if the Account suffered default *and* the Guarantee Fund had already been exhausted by previous calls. The scheme is predicated on the assumption that potential investors would regard this as a sufficiently remote contingency to treat the bonds as low-risk assets, for which they would therefore be prepared to pay a high price. Since a high issue price implies a low interest cost to borrowers, the scheme would in that case be attractive to potential borrowers.

An alternative (or possibly complementary) approach to reassuring creditors would be to require borrowers to take out insurance with an appropriate institution, such as the International Credit Guarantee Fund recently proposed by Witteveen (1981). Since a less creditworthy country would be required to pay a higher insurance premium, this would limit the redistributive impact that would otherwise tend to result from enabling the poorer countries to exploit the creditworthiness of the more advanced. One may or may not welcome such a limitation. If it proved to be necessary to ensure that the more advanced countries realized a positive gain from membership and thus had an incentive to enter, it would be difficult not to welcome it. But if it were merely a mechanism whereby the richer members avoided giving any differential benefits to the less fortunate, some might regret it. An additional and less ambiguous benefit is that the danger of provoking rising insurance premiums would introduce a continuous pressure on countries to correct policy mistakes at an early stage and to avoid excessive financing of deficits that needed adjustment.

(e) Issue arrangements

Issues might take place once a quarter. That would seem to offer adequate flexibility to borrowing countries, while ensuring that if the scheme were even moderately successful there would be homogeneous bond issues of several billion SDRs, which is quite enough to support a vigorous secondary market.

Presumably all developing countries would be entitled to join the sponsoring institution and to borrow by participating in the proceeds of a bond issue. Given the fact that investor attitudes would be influenced by their perceptions of the creditworthiness of the countries whose credit stood behind each issue of bonds, it would be important to ensure that no issue was unduly dominated by a single borrower, and also that no borrower was led to believe that it could set off down the primrose path of borrowing what it could never hope to repay. At the same time, it is surely clear by now that the time is past when most developing countries could (or should) be expected to accept detailed supervision, either of individual projects or of macro-economic policies, as a condition for the receipt of capital inflows on essentially commercial terms. The problem is to design arrangements that will reconcile these conflicting desiderata.

Consider first the problem of how to bar an irresponsible strategy of borrowing more than can be serviced in the expectation of borrowing ever more to pay the accruing debt service.[2] The natural approach is to place an upper limit on the amount that can be borrowed, which should be related to the country's debt-servicing capacity. Since these bonds have been designed to limit debt-service payments, and since output rather than exports is the more relevant criterion of debt-servicing capacity in the long run (when opportunities exist for transforming output into net exports), the best of the usual statistical criteria of debt-servicing capacity would in the present context seem to be the ratio of debt to GDP. Then the international community might determine a maximum acceptable debt:GDP ratio of ρ. A country's maximum borrowing entitlement (E) would then be given by the formula:

$$E = \rho(\text{GDP}) - D$$

where D is total current external debt. This formula would allow countries with modest debt levels to increase their overall indebtedness through the scheme, while countries with debt already close to the level ρ, reckoned to be the maximum consistent with prudence, would be restricted to (i) funding outstanding debt in other, presumably shorter-term, forms, and (ii) increasing borrowing in line with the growth of GDP. Given that the debt-service levels implied by 50-year indexed bonds would be very modest, it would presumably be possible to set ρ at a level that would not seriously constrain the borrowing possibilities of even heavily-indebted countries at the present time. Knowledge that borrowing would come up against such a limit before long would none the less be important in reducing the attractions of irresponsible spendthrift strategies.

Within the limits determined by E, one would presumably wish to leave individual countries basically free to determine the extent of their borrowing each quarter. The extent to which they would wish to exercise those borrowing rights could, of course, be expected to depend upon the issue price of each bond series: if the issue price were high so that the implied real interest rate were low, most countries would wish to borrow more (in part so as to retire more short-term debt) than with a low issue price and thus high interest rate. There is a simple way in which the Sponsor could take appropriate account of national preferences in this respect, and that is to invite potential borrowers to submit in advance of each issue a statement of how much they would wish to borrow at each issue price. Those supply (of bonds) schedules could then be summed and compared with demand, which could be determined each quarter by the Sponsor inviting sealed bids on a certain day. The number of bonds issued would then be determined by the condition that demand be equal to supply. All demand-side bids above the equilibrium price would be satisfied, as would (subject to the qualification noted in the next paragraph) all supply-side offers below the equilibrium price. (See the demand and supply curves D and S in Fig. 7.1.)

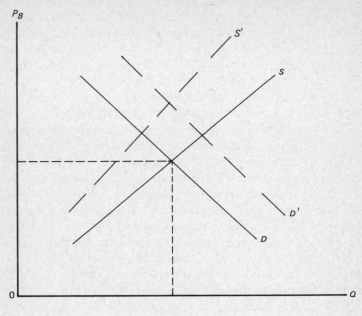

Fig. 7.1

A consequence of organizing issues in this way is that lenders would not know the identity of the borrowing countries whose credit would stand behind a particular issue at the time that they had to submit bids.[3] That would be a significant deterrent to bidding if there were any chance that a particular issue might be dominated by a limited number of borrowers, at least in the absence of a requirement that borrowers take out insurance as discussed at the end of the previous section. It would therefore be desirable to ensure that each bond issue represented a good spread of risks. That could be accomplished by providing that no country should be permitted a share in any bond issue greater than, say, three times its share in the combined GDP of the group of potential borrowers.

The effects of this amendment can be appreciated in terms of Fig. 7.1, which shows the demand and supply curves for a particular forthcoming bond issue. D and S represent what demand and supply would be without the risk-spreading restriction discussed in the previous paragraph. The effect of that restriction would be to prune back the bids submitted by certain countries that had put in particularly high bids relative to GDP, to give a new supply curve S'. The assurance this would give investors as to the spread of risks represented by a new bond issue would shift the demand curve right to D'. The net result would be an unambiguously higher issue price, i.e. a more favourable interest rate to borrowers, while the quantity of bonds issued might either increase or decrease.

(f) Debt service

The Sponsor would have a contractual obligation to pay bond holders a sum determined by the indexation formula described in (c) above. That would determine the sum that the Sponsor would need to raise from the countries that had participated in the particular bond issue in question, assuming there had been no default. In the event of a default, the Sponsor would draw on the Guarantee Fund for the sum that would have been due from the defaulter(s).

There is, of course, a very simple way in which to determine how much each borrower should pay the Sponsor to cover its debt-service obligations, and that is to make the obligation proportionate to the sum borrowed under a particular issue. A country that received 5 per cent of the proceeds of an issue would pay 5 per cent of the cost of debt service, be it for interest or amortization, determined by the indexation formula.

However, it would also be possible to devise a more sophisticated solution involving a measure of risk-sharing between borrowers, thus benefiting them and incidentally — by further reducing the incentive to default — reassuring lenders. The basic idea would be to make the burden of debt-servicing falling on a country vary with its ability to pay — not by making rich countries pay more, which would simply tend to drive them out of the scheme and thus increase the cost the poor would have to pay, but by making obligations vary with the *unpredictable* part of capacity to pay. A good variable to use for this purpose is the terms of trade. Thus an improvement in a borrower's terms of trade would *ceteris paribus* lead to an increase in its debt-service obligation, while a worsening would qualify a country for relief. In order to safeguard the solvency of the Sponsor, it would be necessary to normalize terms-of-trade changes relative to those of the weighted average for the group of borrowers involved in a particular issue. And in order to avoid giving an incentive to countries to borrow when their terms of trade were abnormally favourable, it would be necessary to take as the initial terms of trade from which subsequent changes would be calculated an estimate of the *normal* terms of trade, rather than the *actual* terms of trade at the time the bonds were issued. Obviously the viability of this proposal depends on borrowers showing sufficient good-will to accept the Sponsor's estimates of the 'normal' terms of trade. If that goodwill were present, a scheme like this could be quite useful in cushioning countries against major changes in the terms of trade. For example, had such a scheme been operational at the time of the 1973 oil price increase, the terms of trade changes that actually occurred would have more than doubled the interest obligations of OPEC members and roughly halved those of all other countries on an issue where OPEC was responsible for a quarter of the borrowing, assuming that interest obligations were proportionate to normalized terms of trade changes.[4]

The above scheme would seem entirely appropriate for calculating interest obligations, but perhaps not for repayment of the principal. It would not always be fair to make that burden dependent on the accident of what the terms of trade happened to be on the particular date when repayment fell due. One solution would be to substitute the 'normal' for the actual terms of trade on the repayment date. Another solution would be to amortize over a period of, say, five years, so as to iron out chance fluctuations. A third possibility might be to measure variations in the capacity to pay by a less volatile variable than the terms of trade, such as GDP. A disadvantage of that solution would be that changes in GDP are to some extent foreseeable (whereas changes in the terms of trade are pretty random, as those who have claimed to detect historical trends have found at the cost of their intellectual credibility), which might deter the participation of the potential high-growth countries. Since these are likely to be the countries regarded as most creditworthy by the market, one might again court the danger of creating a 'market for lemons'. My own preference would be to select the second solution and amortize over five or ten years.

3. Concluding remarks

The proposal developed in this chapter might be summarized as one for having an international financial institution act as agent for a collective of developing countries in floating long-term indexed bonds. It is intended to fill one of the two lacunae in present LDC borrowing facilities diagnosed by the Brandt Commission (1980, chaps. 14 and 15), namely, that for long-term programme lending. The emphasis in developing the scheme has indeed been placed on enabling developing countries to undertake general borrowing on long-term maturities without exposing themselves to unreasonable costs and risks. The interests of lenders have entered the analysis essentially as a constraint, as something that must be satisfied if they are to provide the funds that the developing countries need. This presentation reflects where the chapter was written more than who could be expected to benefit by adoption of its proposals. Had I been sitting in Kuwait rather than Rio de Janeiro, I would have argued that OPEC investable funds should be directed in substantial part at the areas promising high rates of return, i.e. the developing countries; that the need to earn a positive real return from those investments without jeopardizing the creditworthiness of the borrowers points to the need for indexed long-term bonds; that the lenders have a strong interest in risk spreading designed to minimize the chances of default, to the point where it would be worth their while donating a certain amount to a Guarantee Fund designed to ensure that default by one borrower did not create pressures on others to follow suit; and so on. In other words, the 'why' would have been different, but the 'how' would have been much the same.

While the low-absorbing oil exporters who need a safe and profitable investment outlet, and preferably one calculated to promote development, are the most obvious target for sales of the indexed bonds discussed in this chapter, they are by no means the only potential buyers. In addition, one would anticipate significant demand from some Western buyers, most particularly from pension funds with their long-term liabilities to whom the guaranteed positive long-term real yield would surely be attractive. More generally, any financial institution with an interest in diversification and an ability to ride out short-term capital losses should be attracted to put a part of its portfolio into an asset that promises such low covariance between its return and that on the existing array of financial assets.

The creation of a mechanism capable of fostering large-scale long-term capital movements from the OPEC surplus states and the developed West to the developing South appears to be one of those rare instances of a genuine harmony of international economic interests. The OPEC surplus countries would benefit from the availability of an investment medium tailored to their needs; the South would benefit from the enlarged availability of real resources with which to accelerate development on terms that would permit the prudent acceptance of larger inflows; the West would benefit from an end to the nagging worries that liquidity difficulties by a major LDC borrower might spark a financial panic and that the commercial banks may prove unable to sustain recycling on the necessary scale indefinitely; and all would benefit by the cyclical stabilizing properties that inhere in a large volume of long-term debt. It is rare to find a potential reform where the only losers would be those wishing disaster on others in the hope of pickings from the carcass. This is surely the type of proposal that is needed to transform the phrase 'new international economic order' from slogan to programme.

Notes

1 Realism compels one to recognize that if the major Western aid donors do not soon improve on their recent dismal performance, inter-donor equity is liable to lead to a downward revision of that figure before the question becomes relevant to many new graduates.
2 In technical terms, the object of the exercise is to rule out paths that violate the transversality conditions.

3 One can, of course, envisage ways of changing that, for example by replacing auctions with sealed bids by tap issues, but that alternative has its own problems of maintaining inter-borrower equity and inflexibility.

4 In terms of a formula, one can say that country i's interest obligation as a share (s_i) of the total interest bill would be:

$$s_i = \frac{T^i_t/T^i_0}{T_t/T_0} \cdot v_i$$

where T^i_t = terms of trade of country i at time t;

T^i_0 = 'normal' terms of trade on issue date of country i;

T_t = weighted average terms of trade of all borrowers at time t, with weights given by v_j;

T_0 = weighted average 'normal' terms of trade of all borrowers on issue date, with weights given by v_j;

$v_i(v_j)$ = proportion of bond issue accounted for by country $i(j)$.

References

G. Akerlof, 'The Market for "Lemons" '; *Quarterly Journal of Economics*, August 1970.

Drandt Commission, *North South: A Programme for Survival*, MIT Press, 1980.

D. Jaffee and E. Kleiman, 'The Welfare Implications of Uneven Inflation', in E. Lundberg, ed., *Inflation Theory and Anti-Inflation Policy*, Westview Press, 1977.

W. A. Lewis, *The Evolution of the International Economic Order*, Princeton University Press, 1978.

P. Volcker, 'The Recycling Problem Revisited', *Challenge*, July/August 1980.

J. Williamson, 'Transferência de Recursos e o Sistema Monetário Internacional', in *Estudos sobre Desenvolvimento Econômico*, BNDE, Rio de Janeiro, 1977.

H. J. Witteveen, 'Proposal for Creating an International Credit Guarantee Fund', mimeo, 27 January 1981.

8 DEVELOPMENT FINANCE IN THE NINETEEN-EIGHTIES

Vijay Joshi

1. Introduction

The case for international public action to increase the volume and improve the terms of capital flows to the poor countries has two distinct strands, one based on altruism, the other on mutual self-interest.

The altruistic argument proceeds from a value judgement regarding the desirability of international redistribution from rich to poor countries. It assumes that living standards in the poor countries should increase at an acceptable minimum rate for humanitarian reasons. It implies that if the economic prospects of the poor countries worsen, and especially if these prospects worsen for reasons beyond their control, aid flows should be stepped up.

The argument from mutual self-interest is of a quite different variety and is based on the idea that increased capital flows to the poor countries would be to the economic advantage of all countries, rich and poor alike. The suboptimal quantity and quality of capital flows are attributed to some form of market failure. This argument, in turn, could be elaborated in two different ways, one of which I find more persuasive than the other:

(i) There is a Keynesian, macro-economic version of the argument, espoused for example by the Brandt Report, which claims that 'massive transfers' to the poor countries would increase employment and output not merely in the poor countries but also in the rich industrial countries as well, through the increased demand generated for the exports of the latter. I do not myself belief that this argument has much practical application. It assumes falsely that expansion in the industrial countries is constrained by the fear of balance of payments deficits; in fact such expansion is constrained by the fear of inflation.

(ii) There is a more orthodox, micro-economic version of the mutual self-interest argument which claims that the rate of return on capital in many poor countries is high enough to justify much larger capital flows than occur at present. Public intervention is judged to be necessary because the market does not perceive this truth due to some distortion or imperfection in its working. A rather different variant of the same argument emphasizes not so much the inadequate quantity of capital flows to the poor countries, as their erratic nature: the market is sometimes too lax in its attitude and at other times withdraws funds entirely. This leads on naturally to the question of devising appropriate conditionality criteria for public loans.

In this chapter, I shall begin by discussing briefly the need for new international public initiatives in development finance. My contention will be that recent international economic developments have strengthened both the altruistic and the mutual self-interest arguments for public intervention. I shall then discuss the form that such intervention should take, with particular reference to the role of the IMF and the World Bank in this context. The reader should note that for analytical convenience I shall divide the world into three groupings: the capital-surplus oil-exporting developing countries (OEC), the industrial countries (IC), and the non-oil less developed countries (NLDC). This does not, of course, correspond exactly to the poor country/rich country distinction made above. The OEC are rich in quite a different sense from the IC since their present affluence is heavily dependent on their earnings from the exploitation of an exhaustible resource. The rationale for the categories employed in this chapter is that they are relevant from the viewpoint of the distribution of international capital flows. The NLDC are all traditionally capital-deficit countries, the IC are the traditionally capital-surplus countries, the OEC are countries which are capital-surplus in the medium run because their savings are likely to exceed their domestic investment possibilities for some time to come. Of course, some oil-exporting countries are capital-deficit countries but their problems fall outside the scope of this chapter.

2. The need for new public initiatives in developing finance

The basic argument of this section is simple. In the present international conjuncture, the NLDC are in a highly vulnerable position. They are being squeezed by high oil prices, low prices of their export commodities, severe recession in the industrial countries and high real interest rates. If the NLDC are to maintain acceptable growth rates in this environment, their financing needs will be very large. But the prospects for financial flows to the NLDC are not good. The political will behind official flows has weakened. There are fears that the commercial banking system has become over-extended. Though the world capital market performed with remarkable efficiency in the 1970s, there is a non-negligible chance that its basic imperfections will come to the fore in the present stagflationary atmosphere and hamper the smoothness of the recycling process. It is, therefore, vitally necessary to explore new methods of direct and indirect public participation in development finance. We now proceed to a brief discussion of the relevant issues.

(a) The impact of oil price increases, past and future

The oil price increases of the 1970s have obviously increased the NLDC's financial needs sharply. The basic implication of an increase in the real price of oil is a shift of world income over time to the OEC. For any given rate of international redistribution, the *magnitude* of the cut in real expenditure that an oil-importing country has to suffer depends upon the ease with which it can do without imported oil. This depends on how easily it can shift production towards oil and its substitutes and consumption away from oil and its complements. It also depends on how easily it can reallocate resources to improve the current account deficit generated by the oil price increase. The *timing* of the cut in real expenditure depends upon the ease with which the oil-importing country can attract capital flows from the OEC, directly or through the intermediation of the capital market, to enable it to tide over the period of adjustment.

The main internal problem that the NLDC are likely to face in adjusting to the oil price increase is inadequate flexibility in reallocating resources, particularly between the traded and non-traded sectors to bring about favourable changes in the balance of payments on current account. But the success of their adjustment efforts is also critically dependent on two external factors: (i) the form of adjustment undertaken by the IC plays an important role. If the IC adjust by adopting deflationary policies, NLDC adjustment is severely hampered and (ii) NLDC adjustment is made more difficult by the instability, actual or potential, of capital flows, resulting from various imperfections of the capital market. Factors (i) and (ii) are discussed in the ensuing sections.

Some of the low income NLDC (e.g. the low-income African countries) are particularly vulnerable with regard to both the magnitude and timing of expenditure cuts because they suffer from the problems mentioned above to an extreme degree. Many of them are fundamentally weak economies with immobile resources, inadequate infra-structure and primitive technology. The inflexibility of these economies requires that the real income cut be large; the difficulty they experience in attracting capital inflows requires that the cut be immediate. In such economies, international altruism has a large role to play.

Unfortunately, the oil price increase of 1979/80 is potentially even more serious than that in 1973/74. To begin with, the real price of oil fell after the first oil price increase; this time, such an outcome is unlikely. There have of course been some economies in world oil consumption recently but my own guess would be that these changes are reversible and that the effect of the IC recession in reducing the demand for oil has been significantly underestimated. Moreover, the OEC are unlikely to take a passive attitude to a fall in oil's real price. To this end, they are likely to be much more willing than in the 1970s to pursue an active supply management policy i.e. to make conscious, portfolio decisions about whether to leave oil in the ground. Another reason why OEC surpluses are likely to be more resistant in the 1980s compared to the 1970s is the likelihood that their spending policies will be more cautious and restrained.

(b) The impact of stagflation in the industrial countries

Perhaps the most critical influence on the prospects of the NLDC during the present decade will be the economic performance of the IC. It is now fairly certain that, for various reasons, the major IC will not grow faster than about 2 per cent per annum for the next several years. This prospect should not all be attributed to the oil price increase. There are other structural factors reducing the growth rate of potential output, such as the slowing down of the rate of technical progress in the US. In addition, the IC are all concerned about the possibilities of inflation getting out of hand. The worsening of the inflation/unemployment trade-off is itself the result of many complex factors including increased trade union power and sharper disagreement about the just distribution of the national product. Whatever the causes may be, the governments of the IC have embraced a restrictionist philosophy which concentrates on deflation of demand as the main instrument for breaking inflationary expectations and weakening trade union power. Tight monetary policies are being pursued in most IC, to the point where there is a danger of competitive interest rate wars. Such policies are also likely to have a dampening effect on the growth of international liquidity.

These developments could be potentially very damaging to the NLDC in three different ways following from the economic weight of the IC in the world economy and particularly in NLDC exports:

(i) NLDC terms of trade are likely to worsen.

(ii) Deflation in the IC is likely to be transmitted to the NLDC; it is exceedingly unlikely that exchange rate and interest rate changes could neutralize this effect.

(iii) If the NLDC governments attempt to maintain growth rates, in the face of stagnant demand for their exports, they could only do so by running much higher ratios of current account deficits to GNP than hitherto over a substantial period of time. The problem with this strategy is that it is only viable if it can be financed. But IC stagnation reduces OPEC surpluses and, therefore, the funds flowing through the capital market. Moreover, in the absence of substantial public intervention, it is unlikely that the world capital market would perform the recycling function efficiently in a deflationary environment.

(c) *The world capital market: basic imperfections and future prospects*

The benign functioning of the world capital market after the first oil price increase has often been commented on. On closer view, however, it becomes evident that the capital market suffers from various shortcomings. The general presumption underlying criticisms of the world capital market is that it systematically underestimates the substantial unexploited investment opportunities which the NLDC possess. One manifestation of capital market imperfection is the extraordinarily skewed distribution of capital flows. For example, it has been estimated that in 1979 four countries, viz. Argentina, Brazil, Mexico and South Korea, accounted for 60 per cent of outstanding gross euro-market lending and 90 per cent of outstanding net euro-market lending to the NLDC.[1] One would ordinarily have expected the rate of return on capital to be high enough in the middle-income NLDC to justify market lending to be spread fairly evenly over them. The above figures show that even among the middle-income NLDC lending is highly concentrated. Another manifestation of capital market imperfection is the maturity distribution of capital flows which is characterized by an almost complete absence of genuinely long-term loans. Of course, it is natural that long-term loans with fixed nominal interest rates should evaporate in an inflationary environment. The market has responded to this problem by developing short-term floating rate loans rather than long-term indexed loans. Floating rate loans protect the interests of the lenders but at the expense of creating severe cash flow problems for borrowers. If the rate of inflation increases, the 'front-loading' of repayments can increase the real burden on borrowers dramatically in the early years of a floating loan rate. The danger in this situation arises from the fact that random adverse changes in the borrower's position can cause panic and threaten a collapse of credit.[2]

What are the reasons for capital market imperfections? I shall particularly emphasize three of them:

(i) Information Problems: To begin with, there is lack of knowledge on the part of the capital market of investment opportunities in the NLDC. But information problems of a more subtle kind can also arise. The inability of banks to distinguish between 'honest' and 'dishonest' borrowers, combined with lack of effective penalties on sovereign governments which default, leads banks to ration credit on the basis of quantitative limits which can be set at 'safe' levels for all borrowers. In contrast, some observers have claimed that bank lending to the NLDC has been excessive since it is based on the implicit guarantee against bankruptcy extended by international public institutions and IC governments to the banks and their soveriegn customers. I find this doubtful. While banks have indeed expanded lending to certain countries too rapidly at certain times, withdrawal of such lending has been equally rapid when difficulties appear.[3] This does not suggest that banks believe in the implicit guarantees with much confidence. On balance, the information problems lead, in my judgement, to private capital flows to the NLDC being less than they would otherwise be.

(ii) Conservatism and excessive risk-aversion: I have already remarked above on the market's strong bias towards short-term loans. In principle, a series of short-term loans is equivalent to a long-term loan. But the capital market can be unduly cautious about the rollover process. The basic difficulty is that banks tend to apply conservative criteria in assessing risk. They are apt to focus not simply on the borrower's net present value position but also on the cash flow situation, so that short-term liquidity problems can have an exaggerated influence. In so far as the liquidity problems are themselves generated by floating interest rates, the capital market can legitimately be criticized for failing to be flexible enough to introduce indexed loans.

(iii) Official rules and regulations: Some of the deficiency of capital flows may be explained as arising out of governmental interference. For example, in many IC there are restrictions on access to capital markets, the main object of which may well be to protect depositors but which in fact end up by discriminating against NLDC borrowers. There also exist official rules which impose quantitative constraints on lending by financial institutions, e.g. the regulations in the US restricting the proportion of a bank's capital that can be at risk to any single sovereign borrower. Official limitations may also exist on the borrower's side. For example, some governments may restrict borrowing because they are autarkic in their economic philosophy or because they take an unduly pessimistic view about their ability to service the international debt they incur. I would not myself ascribe very much significance to official regulations as a source of capital market imperfection. On the lending side, offshore markets are relatively free of official intervention. On the borrowing side, the acute need for finance would overcome most governments' reticence about borrowing in world capital markets.

We now turn to the prospects for private capital flows in the 1980s. Concern has been expressed that adequate recycling may not take place because the banking system is becoming undercapitalized and because NLDC debt has reached dangerous levels. One must not make the mistake of being too pessimistic. There has been no decline in the capital-asset ratio of the major banks taken as a whole nor has there been an increase in the share of loans to the NLDC in the gross external assets of the banking system taken as a whole. If some banks become undercapitalized, banks which are not 'fully lent' would take their place in expanding international lending; similarly, if some banks reach portfolio limits with respect to particular countries, other banks could step in to lend to these countries, if profitable lending opportunities remain. As for NLDC debt, it has expanded rapidly in *nominal* terms but so have exports, GDP, etc., so that the *debt ratios* have not worsened alarmingly, at least at the aggregate level. This is not to deny that the debt ratios of particular countries have shown a marked deterioration. I do not believe that banking and creditworthiness constraints, in themselves, constitute a grave source of danger. The potential for danger arises from the effect that stagflation and protectionism in the IC would have on the international capital market. If these tendencies continue or worsen, the imperfections of the capital market mentioned above would come prominently to the surface and there could be a serious threat to the stability of capital flows to the NLDC.

3.   International public initiatives: scope and modalities

There are two broad questions concerning international public intervention in development finance which need attention:
(i)   What precisely should such intervention seek to achieve and
(ii)   should such intervention work directly through international public institutions, traditional or new, or indirectly by influencing the behaviour of private sector financial institutions appropriately.
In this section, I shall deal with these and other connected issues.
It would be useful to begin with the distinction suggested in the introductory section. International public intervention could be directed to achieving international redistribution or to correcting departures from efficiency in the international capital market. Taking redistribution first, I shall treat bilateral aid flows as falling outside the scope of this chapter, except to remark that the moral case for an increase in the miserable levels of official development assistance is surely overwhelming at the present juncture. (Official development assistance from the IC is no higher than about one-third of one per cent of GNP.) While the operations of the existing multilateral institutions are to be seen mainly as improving the efficiency of the world capital market, their lending does

have some redistributive element. The scope for strengthening this aspect of their activities through interest subsidies and other means will be commented on in a later section. As for private sector financial institutions, they cannot be expected to concern themselves with international redistribution. Of course, in principle, interest subsidies could be disbursed to private sector banks to enable them to make loans at low rates. The standard objection to interest subsidies, in which there is a good deal of force, is that the purpose can be achieved more simply and directly by unrequited grants equal in value to the interest subsidies. There are other objections as well. As with any subsidy, part of the benefit would accrue to the 'producers' (in this case the banks) rather than the 'customers' (in this case the ultimate borrowers). Moreover, interest subsidies may distort the signals for resource allocation in the borrowing countries by making capital 'too cheap'. Interest subsidies to private sector banking loans may, however, have some advantages. They may encourage greater mutual familiarity between the NLDC and the capital market. It is also possible that some donor governments may prefer to see aid channelled in this way rather than as a direct grant.

Turning to international public intervention designed to correct capital market failures, I shall not dwell on the macro-economic international Keynesian version of the argument. It may well be true that the pressure of aggregate demand in the IC is too low even from the viewpoint of their own self-interest but this situation is the product of deliberate choice on the part of IC governments. They cannot be bamboozled into giving up this policy by an expansion of demand for their exports. A reversal of IC demand management policies could only come about as a result of a change in the economic philosophy of the IC governments, not by covert 'international deficit financing'.

The micro-economic version of the market failure argument has greater relevance. There is a presumption that capital flows to the NLDC are inadequate owing to a combination of information problems, excessive risk-aversion of banks and inflexibility of the market in dealing with problems caused by inflation. What should the international public response to these problems be? I shall now discuss three possible remedies: insurance, penalties and indexation.

Insurance schemes

One possible method of dealing with the above problem would be to set up an international insurance agency which would insure private sector loans to the NLDC on payment of a premium. This method may well increase capital flows without increasing interest rates because the insurance premium would be offset by the reduced cost due to spreading of the risk. Setting up such an insurance fund would, however, pose formidable difficulties. It is most unlikely that such an institution could function on the basis of the premia alone. It would need a guarantee fund to cover the risks of bad loans particularly in the early stages and it is difficult to see such a fund being spontaneously generated by the market. IC and OPEC governments would have to step in to provide the guarantees though the proportion of callable to paid-in capital could probably be quite high. When the institution gets going it could take up insurance business considerably in excess of the guarantees. The existence of the guarantee could create a 'moral hazard problem' i.e. it could induce the banks to make unsound loans in the expectation of being compensated in the event of loss. This problem can be met to an extent by guaranteeing only a specified proportion of each loan and, in particular, by making the continuation of insurance cover subject to performance criteria. Another problem which this scheme, like other schemes to increase capital flows, is subject to, is to the 'switching problem'. The question is whether the provision of guarantees would simply lead to the substitution of guaranteed for unguaranteed loans without any additionality. My feeling is that additionality can only be secured if the guarantee scheme is substantial and large in relation to existing capital flows.

Penalties and retaliation

There is another possible way of reducing the risk arising out of lack of information about the creditworthiness of borrowers. It has been suggested that severe penalties be imposed on governments which default, in the form of exclusion from future borrowing and, going further, economic retaliation of other varieties.[4] The idea is that this would reduce the incentive to default, increase the security of the loans which banks make and, consequently, increase private capital flows. Such a proposal would clearly require that international public institutions operate a monitoring and penalty-imposing apparatus. Quite apart from the political problems that such a proposal would involve, it is not even clear that in its crude form it is efficient from an economic point of view. Imposing penalties could conceivably make sense only as a response to irresponsible economic policies by borrowers. But defaults may sometimes be forced on borrowers by uncontrollable events.

Indexation

One of the imperfections of the world capital market isolated above was its insufficient flexibility in dealing with the effect of inflation on capital flows, particularly long-term loans. Proponents of indexation believe. that only indexed assets can balance the interests of lenders and borrowers in a fair manner. The real value of OPEC assets was eroded substantially in the 1980s. They are unlikely to be so amenable during this decade; unless they are offered protection of the real value of their assets, they may choose to leave oil in the ground, which may affect both the IC and the NLDC adversely. As far as borrowers are concerned, indexation would avoid the 'front-loading' problem; we have seen that this problem can have serious effects in an imperfect capital market.[5] The current situation is reasonably favourable for the introduction of indexed assets. We seem to be entering upon a period of positive real interest rates. The borrowing countries cannot be sure that negative real interest rates will return nor can the lending OPEC be sure that real interest rates will remain at present high levels. Hence, there would appear to be real scope for the introduction of indexed assets with a real interest rate of say 1 per cent, in return for an agreement that the real price of oil would rise very moderately and predictably.

The role of international public institutions

The foregoing discussion should make clear that public intervention has to take the form of a judicious mixture of financial provision, financial innovation and monitoring of economic performance. The presumption must be that these tasks are sometimes more efficiently performed by public institutions directly than by indirect support to private institutions. We have seen that the information and risk problem in the private sector can be mitigated by setting up insurance agencies. But it may be easier to achieve the same aim by expansion of the activities of public intermediaries. The same argument applies to the introduction of indexed assets. As for penalties, they would be politically unacceptable in an extreme form. But some approximation to their beneficial effects could be achieved by the conditionality provisions attached to the loans of international public institutions. Neither governments putting up guarantees nor ultimate lenders buying the liabilities of international financial intermediaries are likely to feel secure unless they are convinced that there is monitoring of the adjustment efforts of ultimate borrowers. Public institutions are often in a better position to achieve this than private institutions. There remains a further question, however. Should the expansion of public lending occur through the traditional institutions (principally the IMF and the World Bank) or should it be achieved by setting up a *new* institution?

New vs. old intermediaries

One of the simplest ways to achieve increased recycling would be through the traditional institutions, e.g. by increasing the IMF's quotas and the World Bank's capital. If, in addition, the IMF entered the market directly and the World Bank were to change its gearing ratio, quite sizeable funds would be unlocked. If the political will were present, these changes could be achieved fairly swiftly, probably faster than getting a new institution off the ground. Moreover, there would be significant economies in extending the existing institutions rather than setting up new ones, in view of the fact that the existing institutions have already built up a stock of relevant expertise. The case against the traditional institutions is that (a) they are stuck in old grooves, the IMF in short-term lending and the World Bank in project lending from which they would find it difficult to escape, and (b) they have a decision-making structure that is heavily weighted in favour of the IC. Taking (a) first, it must be noted that there have recently been several new initiatives in the IMF and the World Bank which show willingness to be flexible. These changes could be further extended. Perhaps the complaint against the traditional institutions is fundamentally to do with the existence of conditionality provisions. But even in a new institution, the creditors are unlikely to put up any money if the conditionality is too soft. Turning to (b), it is certainly possible to imagine a new institution with a different voting structure, along the lines, for example, of the International Fund for Agricultural Development in which voting power is equally divided between IC, OPEC and NLDC governments but decisions on some issues require bigger majorities than on other issues. The question is, what are the chances of IC and OEC governments being willing to contribute to a new institution with substantial capital and a 'radical' voting structure, if the presumption is that it is in business to make loans to the NLDC with soft conditionality? The chances are small. There may be greater likelihood of persuading IC and OPEC governments to contribute to setting up affiliates of the IMF or the World Bank with a somewhat modified voting structure. I conclude that realistic multilateral initiatives would have to take place within the IMF/World Bank arena and I now turn to examining the role of these two institutions.

4. The IMF and development finance

The orthodox view is that the IMF should be concerned purely with short-term balance of payments adjustment and keep its hands off long-term development finance. This view can be challenged. Current account adjustment to external shocks such as the oil price increase does, of course, have to occur but this statement leaves open what the speed of adjustment should be. The argument in favour of IMF involvement in longer-term lending than hitherto is two-fold: (a) that many of the existing balance of payments deficits of the NLDC are caused by external, irreversible factors which require a long period of adjustment, and (b) that even if lending is long-term, unexploited investment opportunities in many of the capital-poor NLDC would make it possible for them to repay the loans at market rates. (On this view, the paucity of market lending is due to 'market failure'.)

IMF resource and credit facilities

In the present world situation, the IMF's mix of resources available for lending and the conditionality attached to that lending leaves something to be desired. NLDC quotas amount to SDR 19 billion. Theoretically, this implies access to the IMF of more than SDR 120 billion if all IMF facilities are added together. This is, however, an enormous over-statement. Usable, convertible currencies at the disposal of the IMF amount to about SDR 35 billion. Allowing for IMF lending to the IC and for a safe margin of reserves, realistic, total access of the NLDC to IMF credit would be about SDR 20 billion. In fact, the situation has been somewhat improved by the IMF's recent decision to borrow SDR 6–7 billion per year for the purpose of relending. Nevertheless, this volume of resources is small compared to NLDC financing need over the near future. Even with favourable assumptions regarding IC growth, the cumulative NLDC current account deficit net of expected flows of official development aid, could easily be SDR 250 billion over the next five years. Indeed, with realistic assumptions about IC growth, it could be substantially larger. In such a situation, the IMF could be very short of lendable resources at a time when the world capital market is least able to cope. In my opinion, increasing the resources of the IMF is a much more important issue than softening the conditionality of IMF loans which has attracted a good deal of attention. Of course, even if the conditionality is tough, it should not be en-capsulated in mechanical formulae. Moreover, making the continuation of lending conditional upon satisfactory economic performance is compatible with making larger and longer-term loans than the IMF has hitherto done. To this end, the following changes are urgently necessary:

(i) a substantial increase in the IMF quotas

(ii) further liberalization of the compensatory financing facility, making drawings available for shortfalls lasting more than a year, calculating shortfalls in real terms and allowing drawing for shortfalls caused by rising import prices and

(iii) further liberalization of the extended fund facility by extending the financing period from 3 to 6 years and the repayment period from 10 to 15 years.

SDR creation

It has become intellectually fashionable to downgrade the role of the IMF in creating international liquidity in the current international environment characterized by high capital mobility. But SDR creation remains important for the NLDC. Some NLDC have negligible opportunities for acquiring reserves by borrowing: in this respect, many of the IC are much luckier in that they can accumulate reserves by simple changes in monetary policy. Even for those NLDC which can borrow, however, there is the disadvantage that the loans not only have to be serviced but amortized; and as we have already seen, in an imperfect capital market, refinancing is always a somewhat uncertain matter. SDRs, on the other hand, have the enormous advantage that while net users have to pay interest on them, they do not have to be amortized. It should be noted that the value of world trade and the value of payments imbalances have gone up sharply compared to what was predicted when the decisions concerning SDR allocations in the third Basic Period (SDR 4 billion per year from 1979–83) were made. It is further expected that payments imbalances will continue to be very large for several years beyond 1982. International liquidity will obviously have to increase to accommodate these developments and, for the reasons given above, there are good reasons why the share of SDRs in international liquidity should be at least maintained and preferably increased. On this basis, there is a good case for increasing the supply of

SDRs by SDR 6 billion — 10 billion per year over the next few years.

Going further, there is a good case at the moment for the SDR link, i.e. for allocating the whole of the increase in SDRs to the NLDC or, at any rate, allocating SDRs to the NLDC in a higher proportion than implied by their quotas. The case does not rest on increasing aid through the link. Now that the interest rate on the SDR has been raised to equality with market deposit rates, the aid element in the SDR has almost entirely vanished. The case for the Link now consists principally in its being a more efficient recycling device than private capital flows especially for the low-income NLDC since their capital market access is both limited and subject to the uncertainties of refinancing.

5. The World Bank and development finance

The World Bank is, of course, the most important international public institution concerned with development finance. An important feature of the World Bank lending is its project-oriented and hence slow-disbursing character. Under present circumstances, this feature may be undesirable and the first question is to what extent the World Bank can change the character of some of its leading.

Structural adjustment loans

Under its articles of agreement, the World Bank is empowered to make programme loans which can be disbursed quickly. In the last three years, these have, however, constituted only about 4 per cent of World Bank lending. In the present climate, there is an obvious attraction to the idea of increasing such 'structural adjustment loans'. They would be especially useful if used in conjunction with loans from the IMF's extended fund facility to enable well articulated adjustment and growth strategies lasting several years.

There are three difficulties with expansion of structural adjustment loans. One difficulty which is often mentioned is the lack of expertise in the World Bank to evaluate structural adjustment programmes. This is most implausible. There is certainly no reason to believe that the World Bank is not equipped for the task, at any rate in conjunction with other international agencies. The major difficulty undoubtedly concerns resource availability. Expansion could only be at the expense of the World Bank's valuable project lending activities. The recent increase in the World Bank's capital does, however, open up an opportunity in this respect. World Bank sources have indicated that it should be possible easily to increase structural adjustment lending to $1 billion per year. In quantitative terms, this is a small sum but it could have a large impact if directed to the right places, by improving the creditworthiness of the recipient countries and thereby improving the prospects for private lending. A third difficulty with structural adjustment loans is that they are bound to raise the question of the conditionality provisions on such loans. As with IMF loans, my opinion is that borrowing countries would be more willing to accept strict conditionality provisions if the volume of lending is generous.

Co-financing

Another suggestion which has often been voiced concerns the possibility of World Bank co-financing with the private sector. In principle, the availability of World Bank project preparation and supervision should make banks, which are often not very well informed about the NLDC, interested in co-financing. This could increase the quantity and improve the maturity of private capital flows.

So far, private co-financing with the World Bank has been very small, about $½ billion in 1979. World Bank involvement does involve problems for both borrowers and co-lenders. The cost of World Bank project preparation and supervision has to be covered and World Bank methods and project preparation are often different and more exacting than those of private banks. Ultimately, whether co-financing results in additionality of capital flow depends on whether banks perceive World Bank involvement as reducing their risks significantly. It has been suggested that one way to reduce private risks is to strengthen the cross-default clause so that a default against the co-lender is counted as a default against the World Bank. There are, however, political limits to how much strengthening of the cross-default clause the World Bank can realistically entertain. On balance, it is very doubtful whether co-financing would produce additionality in the absence of a World Bank guarantee of the loans.

It can be expected that World Bank guarantees of private loans would result in additionality of capital flow. The difficulty is that under the World Bank's articles of agreement, its guarantees count fully against its lending limits, so that guarantees could only be at the expense of other lending. One possibility in this context is the extension of partial guarantees which may suffice to attract new lenders who have so far been put off by the credit risk of lending to the NLDC but who do not face the problem of having already accumulated a substantial amount of NLDC debt in their portfolio.

It is evident, however, that the World Bank can make a quantitatively significant difference to the working of the world capital market only if its overall lending capacity is significantly increased. The World Bank has recently had a capital increase, expanding its lending capacity to $80 billion which will permit it to increase its lending in real terms by 5 per cent per annum over the next five years. Some of this could be set aside for a partial guarantee-cum-co-financing programme and for structural assistance lending. If the World Bank secures agreement of member countries for a change in its gearing ratio to say 1:2, the potential for such new departures by the World Bank would obviously be significantly increased.

More radical proposals involving the IMF and the World Bank

Earlier in this chapter, I made an attempt to isolate the market failures afflicting the world capital market which would have to be offset by the activities of the international public institutions. In that vein, one can imagine the IMF and/or the World Bank undertaking measures which are outside their traditional sphere of operations. Various suggestions have been made and I list some of them below. One can of course imagine some of these suggestions being implemented by a brand-new international institution but

I have already given reasons for extending the old institutions rather than setting up new ones. (i) The IMF could borrow on world capital markets for the purpose of on-lending to the NLDC.[6] (ii) Another possibility consists of linking recycling to some form of substitution account. For example, the OPEC could exchange the dollars they earn for SDR-denominated assets issued by the IMF; the dollars themselves could be on-lent by the IMF to the NLDC.[7] (iii) Still another possibility consists in the IMF or the World Bank sponsoring, or even more radically issuing, indexed assets for sale to the OPEC and lending the proceeds to the NLDC.[8] (iv) Affiliates of the World Bank could be set up which differ from the parent institution in having a modified voting structure and being more highly geared. Relevant possibilities include the Energy Affiliate and what has been termed the 'Bank's Bank', the latter functioning with a capital-asset ratio akin to a commercial bank.

In all such schemes, the obvious problem is who would bear the risk involved. It may be feasible for the IMF and/or the World Bank to bear some of the risk but surely not all of it. The conclusion is inescapable that such schemes would require paid-in and callable contributions from the IC and the OPEC.

The IMF, the World Bank and international redistribution

A brief word is necessary about the possibility of using the IMF and World Bank for international redistribution of income. The main avenue for doing so is interest rate subsidies whose pros and cons have already been discussed. It must be appreciated that interest subsidies are quite expensive and require either an annual stream of income or a capitalized lump sum set aside for the purpose. The cost of giving interest subsidies can be illustrated by the fact that a lump sum interest subsidy fund of $100 would be required to enable $300 to be lent for 25 years at 4 per cent if the market rate of interest is 8 per cent. Are there any possible sources for an interest-subsidy fund, apart from voluntary contributions by governments? (Voluntary contributions raise the question of additionality of aid in a quite direct way.) One possibility which has been canvassed by the

Brandt Report is additional gold sales by the IMF. IMF gold holding amounts to approximately 100 million ounces. The sale of say 10 million ounces could easily create a fund of $3 billion. Another possible source is the proceeds of repayment of IMF Trust Fund loans. The Trust Fund has disbursed more than $3 billion; however, the repayments on these loans will not reach sizeable proportions till the mid-1980s. Turning to the World Bank, its profits during the fiscal years 1979 and 1980 were $400 million and $600 million respectively. There are other potential calls on these profits but a part could obviously be used for the provision of interest subsidies. Repayments of past IDA loans constitute another source for an interest subsidy fund. It must be noted that these schemes would principally benefit the 'blend' countries i.e. those which currently receive a mixture of IBRD and IDA loans. The poorest countries could not afford to borrow from the IBRD with interest rate subsidies in the feasible range.

6. Concluding remarks

The available evidence points to the likelihood of continuing stagnation in the IC leading to the transmission of strongly contractionary impulses to the NLDC. In such an atmosphere, the imperfections of the world capital market could be exacerbated and capital flows to the NLDC may fall below tolerable levels of adequacy. In order to mitigate the harshness of this effect, active steps need to be taken to promote the recycling of funds through international public institutions. I have discussed in this chapter the modalities of doing so.

Notes

1 See T. Millick, 'Euro-market recycling of OPEC Surpluses: Fact or Myth', *The Banker*, January 1981.
2 The reasons and remedies for the impact of inflation on capital flows have been brilliantly analysed in John Williamson's paper in this volume.
3 For evidence see B. Nowzad and R. Williams, 'External Indebtedness of Developing Countries', IMF Occasional Paper No. 3.

4 For example see J. Eaton and M. Gersovitz, 'Poor Country Borrowing in Private Financial Markets and the Repudiation Issue', Discussion Paper No. 94, Woodrow Wilson School, Princeton University.
5 See Williamson, op. cit.
6 The demand for loans from the IMF has been extremely buoyant in 1980 and 1981. Unless the Eighth Revision of Quotas is brought forward, it seems unlikely that the IMF can meet the legitimate demands of its members without borrowing from the market.
7 See Lal Jayawardena's chapter in this volume.
8 See John Williamson's chapter in this volume.

INDEX

Agriculture, investment levels, 13
Algeria, proposal for OPEC aid body, 15, 16–17, 25, 50, 119–20, 123
Arusha programme for collective self-reliance, 24, 26, 35
Austrian Government Guaranteed Loan (1923–43), 58

Balance of payments, financing structural change, 47–8; IMF and adjustments, 170–1; OPEC Special Fund, 25, 26, world effect of OPEC surpluses, 63; zero sum of surpluses and deficits, 36; see also Deficits; Surpluses
Banking sector, capital to assets ratio, 41–2, 113–14, 164; co-financing with World Bank, 174–5; concern over OPEC surpluses, 63–4; decline in rate of lending, 41; effects of increased OPEC deposits, 43–4; exposure to recycling risks, 11; fear of inability to continue recycling, 40–1; finance for mineral exploration, 7; loan interest subsidies, 166; receiving liquid deposits from OPEC countries, 72; role in freezing foreign assets, 67; role in recycling, 23, 37; role of private banks in resource transfer, 2, 113–15
Bayerische Vereinsbank, 42
Brandt Commission, 124, 153; consideration of new institution for 'massive transfer' of resources, 53; World Development Fund proposed, 47; see also World Development Fund
Brazil, problem of debt-service ratio, 137
Bretton Woods system, important features, 18–19; oriented to developing countries, 18; still apparent

in current systems, 18; support for single financial organization, 48
Burgess, Randolph, 48

Capital flows, lack of political will to encourage, 159; private, in 1980s, 164–5; reasons for encouraging, 157; reasons for sub-optimal performance, 157–8; role of public institutions, 169; see also Recycling surpluses
Capital markets, imperfections, 162–3; see also International financial institutions
China, joins International Monetary Fund, 12
Commerzbank, 42
Commodity stabilization, 5, 13
Cooperation, economic, basic to international financial reforms, 25; failures of present system, 18–23; need for finance to support, 6–7, 13

Debt of LDCs, arranging long-term loans, 137–53; 'burden' relatively stable, 132; disincentive to default, 167–8; finance for reorganization, 13; floating rate loans, 162; guarantees and insurance compared, 145–7; loan arrangement by LDCs collectively, 141; maturity of indexed loans, 142–3; need for refinancing machinery, 9; problems of short maturities, 133; ratio to exports, 132; related to creditworthiness, 136; rollover, 134–5, 163; security problems, 163; see also Indexation of long-term debt
Debt-service payments, 133–4, 151–3; finance for reorganization of, 8–9
Decision-making, by financial institutions, 56–7